A Happy Book

dreamtime

For Nishi,
With affection
and love,
Sammy

Sam Pickering

The University of South Carolina Press

© 2011 University of South Carolina

Published by the University of South Carolina Press
Columbia, South Carolina 29208

www.sc.edu/uscpress

Manufactured in the United States of America

20 19 18 17 16 15 14 13 12 11
10 9 8 7 6 5 4 3 2 1

Library of Congress Cataloging-in-Publication Data
Pickering, Samuel F., 1941–
  Dreamtime : a happy book / Sam Pickering.
      p. cm.
  A collection of personal essays.
  ISBN 978-1-61117-038-2 (pbk : alk. paper)
  1. Pickering, Samuel F., 1941– 2. English teachers—
United States—Biography. 3. American essays. I. Title.
  PE64.P53A3 2011a
  814'.3—dc23

                              2011021256

The author and publisher gratefully acknowledge the
following publications in which essays in this volume
first appeared: *River Teeth* and *Southwest Review.*

Barbara Olds's poem "Promise" is reproduced
through her kind permission.

dreamtime

Other Books by Sam Pickering

Contents

Introduction

Last month I dreamed about a family so famously happy that the government commissioned a study of them. "Unearthing the secret of happiness," the principal investigator said, "would spread blessings around the globe, ending all wars and thus altering the courses of human history and evolution." Accordingly scientists began the study with great enthusiasm and high expectations. Magnetic resonators thumped. Neurologists scanned, and psychiatrists questioned and probed. Hematologists drained quarts of blood, and biologists sequenced DNA, dividing and subdividing, recombining and multiplying, using machines hidden beneath a mountain in Utah, the devices so secret that aside from the investigators only the Central Intelligence Agency knew they existed. Alas, despite the expenditure of a black hole of money and intellectual efforts so intense that three score researchers collapsed and had to be bused to sanitariums to undergo nerve cures, the study failed to reveal the source of happiness. In dreams, and actually in waking life, knowledge depends as much upon happenstance as it does upon planning and investigation. Two months after the study ended, a plumber flushing a pipe running under the basement of the family's home cracked a slab of granite and discovered the house sat atop a river of nitrous oxide.

Laughing gas has drifted misty across my years, some of the zephyrs, I am afraid, generated by the soiled and the bawdy or, as aficionados of southern barnyards know, by bluegrass marmalade. Most of the gas, however, percolates from my character. In "Self-Reliance," Emerson described "the nonchalance of boys who are sure of a dinner." I grew up as one of those boys. I've had a fortunate life. Never have want or mood pinched years into frowns. I have been extraordinarily lucky. As rainbows appear only in the sunshine, so my days have been bright. Consequently this is a happy book, perhaps not one that people unable to shake the burden of thinking themselves burdened will enjoy. The matters I recount are uncomplicated, not like the recollection of the girl whose beloved was a dental student and who, when he traveled across the country on a fellowship, pulled one of her molars so he'd have something to remember her by.

My mind resembles flypaper. Clouds of small doings buzz through my days and stick to consciousness. Names pepper my pages, those of turnips and strawberries, for example, yellow Aberdeen and strap-leaf red-top among the first, lady finger and New Jersey scarlet, Peabody and Scotch runner among the second. I like poking about and compiling lists, say, of things found in an old barn: mole traps, a hay fork, bush hooks, the bottom of a churn, a lightning rod, hog scrapers, and, if a person is sharp eyed, a milk jester or lactometer for measuring butterfat. Teeth, declares an old Roman saying, are shrubs, the roots of which dig below the gums deep into the earth. To keep teeth healthy one must feed and water them, and being an amateur gardener, I write much about food and drink. None of the meals I describe are fancy. Last week Vicki and I ate at Panda Express in the food court on the university campus. We split helpings of fried rice, broccoli beef, and black pepper chicken.

My mind works by association, and thinking about peppered chicken reminds me of the ancient definition of man, a biped without a gizzard. Birds, of course, have gizzards, and I write about birds, indeed about the natural world. Instead of leaning on the everlasting arm, as the gospel song puts it, I kneel on the ground, raking through grasses, searching for caterpillars and spiders. Natural matters are more complex than people usually think. Since I teach at a university, I have the leisure to ponder. The definition of man started me thinking about angels. Although angels are bipeds, they have wings, can fly, and from a distance look like birds, convincing me that they have gizzards, albeit since angels confine themselves to a diet of milk and honey, I assume that lack of use has caused the gizzards to atrophy, like the human appendix. Oddities take flight in my essays. In January I read an article about an entrepreneur who, after losing his position on Wall Street, began breeding ducks with four wings, mallards, I think. In greener economic times, the man had spent a year as a broker in Saudi Arabia and Dubai. Most of his customers were sheiks, and in order to appeal to them and their interests, the man had become an amateur falconer. In comparison to ducks, falcons are rare and expensive. Because of their two sets of wings, the man's ducks were able to rocket through the air, and once the man taught them to snap their bills together and to pluck small birds from the breeze and rabbits from the ground, the man intended to sell the ducks to sheiks, many of whom needed to economize, their "discretionary funds having been adversely affected by the cascading price of oil."

Educational doings swell signatures of my pages. I like teaching and students, but classes, and English departments, have changed from what they were forty years ago. Most of my pals, old boys of legend and sometimes scandal, have retired, their places taken by women or "gals," as the unreconstructed of my generation call them. Most of the women teach well, but they appoint their classrooms differently. "I'll never read another evaluation of my teaching," my friend Irv Davis said at the beginning of this semester. In an evaluation a student complained that "Mr. Davis never brings baked goods to class." "What the hell!" Irv exclaimed. "Chocolate-chip cookies, cupcakes, and ovens sweet and fatty with banana bread! These women have a lot to answer for."

In this book I roam eastern Connecticut and Beaver River, Nova Scotia, where Vicki and I spend summers on farmland her father bought in 1947. Occasionally I wander farther afield, in particular into Mexico and the Caribbean. I meander rather than travel. Youth travels, sucking sulfites out of wineskins and experiencing the ineffable, in the process finding meaning and discovering themselves. Imposing profundity upon hours doesn't interest me, and I have never experienced a crisis of identity. I knew who I was before I clambered from the womb although occasionally when I glimpse myself in the mirror, not something I do much nowadays, I wonder who's the grim, wrinkled stranger glaring at me. I am also a reader, and as I meander wood and field eyes peeled for birds and mushrooms, for whatever swoops into my ken, so I amble libraries, randomly plucking books from shelves, prospecting for glittering nubs of this and that, fool's gold appealing to me more than the twenty-four carat. In the nineteenth century James Vick published a mail-order catalog and sold seeds and plants from a nursery in Rochester, New York. Vick advertised extensively in the *American Agriculturalist*, testimonials from his customers dominating the advertisements. On January 4, 1864, "George Ford" wrote Vick from Lawrence, Kansas, describing how horticulture protected his family and property from the ravages of war. "Please send me your Catalogue for 1864," Ford requested. "The flower seeds we purchased from you last Spring came up remarkably well, much better than those that came from ———. The Asters were very fine, some seventy plants being in full bloom at the time of the Quantrell Raid, and made, together with the Snap Dragons, Dianthus, Heddewigs, Phloxes, Petunias and other fine varieties, a very gay and beautiful appearance, and were the means, providentially, of saving our house from pillage and destruction. Quantrell, with a dozen of his gang, came to destroy the place, but Quantrell said to my wife it was too pretty to burn, and should be saved. Thus you see that the beauty of cultivated nature softened the heart of a notorious bushwhacker and cold-blooded murderer. We shall cultivate flowers as long as we remember this horrible rebellion."

I have aged into the grand medicinal decades, doctors having carved into me four times in five years. As a result lancets chop double edged through several essays, simultaneously painful and tickling. Moreover pharmacology so interests me that I peruse magazines almost as if I were exploring drugstores, their columns stacks of patented advertisements, many hawking wondrous cure-alls. "If taken two days before symptoms appear, Colgan's Apple Water Emulsion never fails to cure Croup, Catarrh, and Constipation." A pediatrician advised parents to follow "French Methodology" in preparing doses of castor oil for their children. "Pour a quarter cup of oil into a sauce pan so that it covers the bottom of the pan. Warm slowly. In a bowl mix the whites from two large eggs, two tablespoons of unsalted butter, and a half a cup of heavy cream. Pour the contents of the bowl into the sauce pan and stir, adding currant jelly to taste. If the consistency is unappetizingly runny, add an eighth of a cup of yellow cornmeal."

Essays are usually short. As the form constricts description and confines rumination to a thin signature of paper, so it distorts the lives of essayists themselves, often making them appear solitaries. I am not a loner, and the clunky gravy of domesticity seasons this book. Vicki and I have shuffled through thirty years together, rarely bruising each other, although I must say that Vicki's skin is more sensitive than mine, rising to purple at the slightest bump. Still our children have grown up and left home, and once or twice melancholy looms over a paragraph like the wolf moon. Still I rarely howl, and nothing melodramatic occurs on my pages. At gray times I lay my pencil down and sit quietly, a dog on my lap despite my not being sure if rubbing a dog decreases or increases melancholy. Incidentally I write about dogs. For some people automobiles bookmark passages of time, for a hardy few a succession of wives or husbands. For my part dogs I've owned mark my years, there being but one gap, this beginning after college and lasting a decade or so, until I, too, became a domestic animal.

No man is Everyman, experiencing all of life, and there are many things I do not write about. Although I describe the doings of a few road races, I write little about sports. I wanted to plug this athletic gap, and in January Vicki and I went to a boys' basketball game at the university.

I was excited as this was only the second game I'd attended in thirty-two years. Unfortunately the game turned out to be a commercial, not a sporting, event; "gymcrackery," Vicki labeled it. Because the game was televised, advertisements broke play into jittering segments, no segment lasting more than two and a half minutes. During intervals the rectangular court became a circus ring. A battalion of twenty-eight cheerleaders pranced across the floor, camouflaged in blue and white sequins. During two breaks they catapulted T-shirts into the audience. A female dance team transformed their backsides into pompoms. A girl shot foul shots, winning fifty dollars. Two small boys raced the length of the court, stopping three times on the way, the first time to put on jerseys that hung on them like curtains, the next to don shorts that hid their feet, and the last to slip into huge shoes, something difficult to accomplish since the shorts kept getting in the way. All the while hip-hop music blared over the public address system or the pep band jangled; surrounding this last, pods of gyrating students, their faces painted blue and white. Attached to the walls of the gymnasium above and behind each backboard was a massive television screen. When the music paused, cameras panned the audience. On seeing themselves on a screen, spectators began jiggling like insects exposed when rocks are turned over, waving their arms like antennae, their mouths mandibles opening and shutting vacuously. Noticing the goings-on in the ring was difficult because advertisements beat a tympani that drummed incessantly across the eyes: Dunkin' Donuts, Travelers with its red umbrella, Bob's Stores, Nike, Toyota, Aspen "Let Us Help You Find Your Smile" Dental, People's United Bank, Big Y "Grocery of the UCONN Huskies," Powers Resort Wear Apparel, AT&T, Connecticut Lottery, ING, State Farm, *Hartford Courant*, WTIC Radio, Supercuts, Channel 8, Liberty Mutual Car & Home Insurance, Mitsubishi Electric, and Muscle Milk flexing the imperative "Drink. Evolve." "Advertisements for everything," Vicki said later, "except Grapevine Cigars and Celia Conklin's Fragrant Cream." "What?" I said. "Celia Conklin's Fragrant Cream," Vicki repeated, "good for chapped hands and face, cracked lips, sunburn, nettle rash, corns, warts, and mosquito bites, a tonic and food for the skin." "How about eradicating clubroot in the cabbage patch?" I said. "That too—everything," Vicki said.

Of course I don't write about a multitude of other things. Music floats "lite" though the book. My memory has gone deaf, and tunes no longer juke across the turntable of my mind. Additionally I don't write about intimate matters, that is, sexual congress, or for that matter any member of the congress family. Indeed the two-lobed congress oozing bile in Washington is probably more pestiferous than any untoward, private species although occasionally the words of a legislator molt and become airborne, as did those of an aspiring congressman from the Volunteer State who recently declared, "The crisis which were about to have arriven have done arroven." In any case plentitude enough exists, something to appeal to or perhaps "bug" sundry readers. When asked to identify the most entomological line in Shakespeare, readers of this book will be able to answer immediately, "Banquo's command to his son in *Macbeth* 'Fly, good Fleance, fly, fly, fly!'" For folks slow to imbibe puns, the line consists of four flies, one flea, and an undetermined number of ants.

In a recent issue of the *London Review of Books,* Frank Kermode wrote, "It is useless to wonder at the ordinariness of exceptionally gifted lives." What isn't fruitless is realizing that exceptional gifts enrich everyone's days. The knack comes in learning to recognize the gifts then to mull them long enough to appreciate them. "People who think they can make me think," an old curmudgeon declared, "had better think again." I don't presume to believe that I can make people think. What I hope is that this book will make some readers smile. Maybe a few people will pause and, glancing about, will marvel at ordinary life. Later, of course, the book will, and should, drop from thought, after which, if the reader is my age, he'll go to bed and, as the saying puts it, will sleep like a top, that is, spend the night turning around and around.

The End of Term

"In the summer," **Wendy began** her final paper for my class on nature writers, "I wake up at seven, eat oatmeal with blueberries, and leave the house on my purple bicycle, wearing a sweatshirt to protect myself from the cold morning air. I ride past tobacco barns and through tobacco fields, sometimes taking my hands off the handlebars to clap and scare a flock of crows into flight. I climb to the top of a giant green hill that was once the city dump but is now covered in wildflowers. I bike fast and get to work before the blueberry farm opens, so I can pin up the bird nets before customers arrive. Everyone talks to me. Old men give me advice about the future. Children talk about how many berries they've picked. Everybody describes their families, their dogs, and their vacations to Maine. For some reason in the middle of the dewy grass and steadily rising July sun, people want to know their neighbors."

The end of the semester is melancholy. Just as I begin to know the students in my classes, they vanish: Wendy amid the blueberries, the boy who paid for his schooling by teaching yoga in New Haven, a professional skateboarder, the two fishing guides, and a girl who had "always" wanted to be a lawyer but who suddenly was unsure and asked plaintively, "What should I do with the rest of my life?" "Talk to your parents," I suggested. "Mother doesn't care what I do," the girl replied, "and I haven't seen my father since I was eight." I've taught for forty years, and the girl's response was more expected than surprising. I looked out my office window. Lilac and autumn olive were sweet in the air. Azaleas were red with horns; and chimes of silverbells shook, then fell silently to the ground. A larch glowed, its limbs the baselines of diagrammed sentences, its new needles flusters of spiky adjectives and adverbs. In distant yards violets wavered fragile and pale, while bugle rose in single blue notes. In the damp leafy woods beyond Horsebarn Hill, ferns thrust into unravelings, and jacks preached from scores of hooded green pulpits.

Along the banks of granite streams, red trillium curtsied demure and humble, while in quiet eddies marsh marigolds burst into bright youthful yellow.

After two girls handed in their last papers at the same time, one lingered in my office. "That girl lives near me," the student said, describing the girl who left. "She's nice, and she eats lots of beets." "My word," I said. "Yes," the girl added as she, too, turned to leave the room, "lots of beets. You can't imagine how many beets." I started reading an essay written by a boy majoring in biology. In the paper the boy traced the life spans of endoparasites infesting cats. Cats, he wrote, for example, excreted the eggs of *Toxoplasma gondii*. The parasite changed the behavior of rodents who fed on the feces of infected cats, making them less wary, even drawing them toward cat urine, increasing the likelihood of their being eaten by cats. Once inside a cat the *Toxoplasma* spawned, the animal eventually excreting the parasite's eggs, continuing, as the boy phrased it, "the happy cycle of life." "Heavens," I said aloud, pausing to open a box on my desk.

The last book students read for my course was *Walden*. The reading coincided with the opening of a restaurant near campus, one specializing in breakfasts and hamburgers, supplemented by a menu of sweet asides, the most striking being deep-fried Oreo cookies. Thoreau wrote that he was determined to know beans, though one day he spiced up a meal with fricasseed woodchuck. The Oreos provided an occasion for me to bounce from Thoreau's "simplicity" into a sermon dragging the shallows of the streams in which we went "a-fishing" and eating. In a fashion my preaching took. To the final class meeting Jessica brought forty deep-fried Oreos. "Perhaps you should try one," she suggested. "Thank you," I said, then demurred, pleading cholesterol. The box atop my desk contained three cookies left over from class. "Just the medication to purge *Toxoplasma gondii*," I thought, seizing an Oreo. I saved the other two cookies for Vicki. "Very good," she said at tea that afternoon. "What was Jessica's grade before she brought these to class?" "B," I said. "Well," Vicki said finishing the second Oreo, "I trust you will give her an A in the course." "Certainly," I said, paraphrasing Thoreau, "she learned that a person should not play at life but should 'earnestly *live* it.'" "Good," Vicki said, "now get on your bicycle and ride over to Storrs Hall and look at the big horse chestnut. The tree is incandescent with spires of white flowers."

For me the annual spring horse auction, held during the last week in April, signals the beginning of the end of term, the heady aroma of manure and hay always making me dream of roaming, if not bounding along astride a quarter horse, at least ambling beside Vicki listening to red-winged blackbirds and anticipating the arrival of warblers. As each new spring differs slightly from every past spring, so each horse auction is unique. This year thirty-eight "lots" were for sale, two mules and a range of horses, Cashmere and Cody, Geronimo, Isis, Airborne, Brandy and Nellie, Jake and Jazz—quarter horses, registered Morgans, paints, an Arabian, an Appaloosa, and a miniature colt that, the auctioneer said, "has a fantastic temperament and gets along well with other farm animals and even likes dogs." The youngest horse on the block was a two-year-old filly, the oldest a thirty-two-year-old gelding. The horses' vaccinations were "current," and all came stapled with microchips for identification. A trio of Connecticut Animal Control officers scrutinized the paperwork of each sale. Attached to the front of the table at which they sat was a notice reading, "If you are acting as a third party to purchase an animal for anyone who is a party to an animal cruelty investigation, there is a potential that you could be violating state law and you could be charged for such violation."

The Connecticut Department of Agriculture's Equine Rescue Program contributed twenty-four lots to the auction, animals not maintained by their previous owners, the number a sign of hard monetary times. The economy affected the auction. Several years back horses sold for $6,000 or $7,000. The top price paid this year was $2,600 for Ovation, a twenty-year-old registered Morgan mare. Ovation probably went to a riding school, one that taught children, for she was "a very honest mare" and, the program stated, "a great lesson horse, both English and Western." Almost half the horses did not sell or meet the minimum, initially $300 for rescue horses although during the sale the man in charge of the horses dropped the price to $200, saying it cost that much to ship a horse back to the state farm. "Take this horse home and put it on your lawn," the auctioneer said while trying to sell a five-year-old paint gelding, "you can't buy a lawn mower for $200." Most university horses that sold brought between $500 (the minimum) and $800. The few horses that went for more than $1,000 were easy riders. Endeavor, a seventeen-year-old registered Morgan gelding, for example, brought $1,500. "Endeavor," the program stated, "is not only adorable, but he is an easy mount. He goes English, Western and loves the trails. Currently, he is doing all of the above, plus he is a star on the Morgan Drill Team. Endeavor is most definitely smart and sensible." The mules sold for $400 apiece. "I don't know what I will do with them," the man who purchased them told me. "I bought them for memory's sake. My grandfather had mules, and I loved him." The sale put a quirt to my imagination. Not only did I dream of buying a horse, but imagination affected my sight, the women most active at the auction, all seeming to have long, horsey hair, not pony tails, but manes, chestnut, palomino, buckskin, and dun with "tiger stripes."

Edward and Eliza accompanied Vicki and me to the auction. Afterward we walked to the university's dairy bar and had ice cream, Vicki, maple walnut, Eliza, cookies and cream, and Edward, chocolate-chip cookie dough. For my part I am "sensitive on mouth" like Nikko, a twenty-six-year-old gelding who sold for $300, and I had good, honest, registered chocolate, a child's cone only a hand high. In the dairy bar was a farmer we had seen at the sale. He had tossed the dietary bit and was also eating chocolate, a massive cup that towered over my cone. He wore a T-shirt on the front of which appeared a picture of four lank-haired Apache braves, all carrying rifles. Stamped above the picture was "Homeland Security," below was the phrase, "Fighting Terrorism Since 1492."

Before leaving the dairy bar, the farmer bought a small cup of vanilla, which he took outside to his truck and fed to an aged Jack Russell perched on the passenger's side of the front seat. Imaginary ties are often real. "He is old and weak like Penny," Vicki said, noticing the dog. Six days later Penny, our Jack Russell, died. Penny was fifteen, the runt and last of a puppy-mill litter when Vicki purchased her. At the time I was out of censorious sight, in Houston mucking out the house of a senile uncle. Vicki had long thought George, our dachshund, needed a canine companion. On the morning I left for Texas, she promised that she would not look at a dog while I was gone. The next day she bought Penny. Five days later, the night before I flew home, Vicki telephoned and said Eliza, who was ten, wanted to speak to me. "Daddy," Eliza said, "we have a surprise for you." What I thought differed from what I said. "That's wonderful, Eliza. Don't tell me what it is, but I'll bet it barks," I said, "I can't wait to see it." Penny was tiny and white, a heartthrob that fell asleep in my lap almost as soon as I walked into the house. Fifteen years is a long time in a person's life. Eliza is no longer a little girl, and nowadays all my surprises are medical and expected rather than suspected.

For a year Penny had staggered toward death, losing sight, hearing, and balance. Yet, three weeks before she died, she accompanied Vicki and me on a walk across the field and into woods below the red barn on the university farm. I carried her through high grass and lifted her over logs and across streams, but she was a trooper, flagging but never stopping. Penny's last fortnight was hard. For a year I had awakened her at six every morning and carried her outside. Once in the yard she walked, even frisked. At the beginning of her last week, however, she broke down and couldn't stand, and whenever I took her out, I supported her. Afterward I brought her inside and, covering her, placed her back in her bed where she stayed until I took her out again. Three days before she died, she became comatose and quit eating. I stopped carrying her out, and four times a day Vicki sponged her off and washed the towels in which she slept. Vicki wanted Penny to die at home, saying that putting her to sleep in a strange place "would be terrible, even though Penny wouldn't know where she was." I wasn't sure, and the morning Penny died, I almost said that kindness was often cruelty. I am glad I said nothing. Four hours later, at 12:36, Penny made a clicking sound and died at home in her bed under the kitchen table, her human family nearby, Vicki five feet away washing a blue bowl in the sink, and I in the study eating peach yogurt, having just returned from jogging.

After finishing the yogurt, I put on work clothes and, going outside, dug Penny's grave in the dell below the study window. The day was dank, and the digging was difficult, the ground being mostly till—gravelly rocks and big stones, roots wrapping through and about them like rope. Once the hole was deep and broad, I shoveled up compost from the woods behind the house. Later I used the compost as fill to replace the stones I removed from the hole, Vicki having said that she "couldn't stand to think of Penny's being crushed by rocks." At four-thirty we buried Penny. We left her collar on, all three children e-mailing Vicki and saying that burying Penny "naked would be awful." Vicki lined the bottom of the grave with an old undershirt, one "familiar with my scent," she said. The burial was pagan but satisfying. Vicki put a chewy toy between Penny's paws, a cross between a squirrel and mouse, slow moving so it could be caught easily but hairy, helping it to endure shaking and tossing. Beside Penny's muzzle, Vicki placed three small dog biscuits shaped like bones and two hunks of Waggin' Train Wholesome Chicken Jerky Tenders. Penny had lost so many teeth she hadn't been able to eat hard food for months. "She'll get new teeth where she is going, and she'll enjoy the jerky," Vicki said. Next we covered Penny with flowers, rose petals from flowers in the house and from outside, daffodils, tulips, streamers of periwinkle, and a carpet of tiny Quaker ladies. Finally I filled the grave with dirt and compost, shaping a mound, into the head of which Vicki stuck a small jar filled with water and containing a bouquet of violets.

The next morning we drove to Ledgecrest and bought perennials. That afternoon we planted them around the grave, Jacob's ladder, forget-me-nots, a deep purple oxalis, and, at the top and bottom, small rose bushes thick with red blossoms.

Not simply season but also the personal links moments and defines a span of time. For me the end of term was in part dog days. Examinations began two days after I buried Penny. That evening when I entered the university library, a sign greeted me. "Paws to Relax," the sign suggested. On the sign appeared a colored picture of a golden retriever sitting in patch of ox-eyed daisies. Under the picture was "Pet therapy dogs to help de-stress during exams" and a list of hours when dogs would be available on level I or level B of the library. Most of the hours were in the afternoon, but some were at night or in the morning. Among the dogs participating in the sessions were Dooley, Jester, Quinn, Luna, Mia, and Savannah. "Darn, this takes all dog," I thought, initially not sure whether to chuckle or sneer. My ambivalence was short lived. I smiled and thought about Penny, the horse auction, and trees blooming on campus, black cherries along the North Eagleville Road, and daphne beside the dairy bar sweeter than any ice cream.

I wanted the end of term to continue into a start. I didn't want to forget the names and faces of my students, so I pondered writing a second book about teaching. *Letters to a Teacher,* my first book on the subject, was gentle and soft, in horse terms "easy to work with" and stood for the farrier. "I'll lay out my final thoughts on teaching," I told Edward. "Good. You'll have to be tough and iconoclastic. How will you begin?" Edward said. "How about, 'When I first started to teach, boys were smarter and girls better looking,'" he continued, answering his own question. "You'll also need a clever title." That night I read a humorous essay by Jerome K. Jerome entitled, "On the Care and Management of Women." A slight emendation gave me a title, "On the Care and Management of Students." "Wonderful," my friend Josh exclaimed, adding that differences between the two groups were slight. "Neither should be allowed to munch wild oats." I smiled, but as I listened to Josh, the end of term ended.

I could have produced a snappy manuscript. But I knew the click and jump of wit would have distorted the delights of deep-fried Oreos as well as of experiences outside the schoolroom, moments that accompanied me to class and shaped my courses. I didn't want to, as Thoreau put it, "suck out all the marrow of life." I was too old for that. But neither did I want to restrict myself to nibbling at the bony edges of existence in order to turn out a book. "I often bike these farm roads again at sunset," Wendy wrote, "when most of the tractors have returned to the barns and the sky is streaked with orange and filled with puffy pink clouds. The silos become dark silhouettes towering over empty fields. The air starts to fill with the sounds of crickets and the twanging calls of bullfrogs that hide in the damp along the road. If I am with a friend, we often get off our bikes and run into a strawberry patch, pick one strawberry, then race away." I suspect Wendy ate more than a single berry. No matter, nothing I wrote about teaching could do justice to a student's pedaling under an orange sky, bullfrogs twanging an accompaniment, maybe a cat howling in the distance, parasites giving it a bellyache, and then perhaps cantering across a shadowy green hill, Maddy, a twenty-year-old paint mare, bought at auction, an "easy to ride" present from a mother to a daughter.

Research

Connecticut takes pride in being a "Tier I" research university, and an archipelago of centers and institutes surrounds the library and athletic fields. Reefs of specialized learning bracket many of the islands, and I have never explored the Institute of Material Science, for example, with its Electrical Insulation Research Center and its Center for Advanced Deployable Nano-Sensors. I pondered wandering into a meeting of the New Literacies Research Team, but then I read that the group concentrated their energies on new information and communication technologies "central to full civic, economic, and personal participation in a globalized community." Unfortunately I inhabit a localized community and have little use for new technologies; old ways of knowing and doing having served me well.

The Center of Excellence for Vaccine Research with its focus on the biology of mycoplasma pathogens intrigued me. Besides being the "etiologic agent of Chronic Respiratory Disease," which costs the poultry business in the United States $700 million annually, *Mycoplasma gallisepticum* "emerged in 1994 as a cause of conjunctivitis in free-ranging house finches in the mid-Atlantic region" of the United States. Anything to do with birds sets me aflutter, and I mulled exploring the center. But then I, too, was a trifle free ranging, if not quite so far wandering as *Carpodacus mexicanus,* and I realized that before being allowed to roam the center I would be subjected to a regimen of inoculations, not something appealing to a person of my mandible.

I do much research, all solidly based on happenstance, my tools curiosity and studious habit. Recently I learned that the first king of Abyssinia was a serpent and that *nilder-nalder* meant dally. "Dirt," I read in a nook in the library, was "only matter in the wrong place." Plumbers in small towns, I discovered this summer, do landfills of business during holidays, especially over Christmas when relatives return from out of state and swell families, not only taxing hospitality but also drains, plugging traps and clogging fittings. Last week I found a broadside pressed between the pages of a hundred-and-thirty-year-old number of the *Rural New Yorker*. Printed on rough rag paper and measuring nine and a half by six inches, the broadside announced the appearance of "Chas. Worcester's Elfin Star Troupe." Admission was twenty-five cents, with children under twelve admitted for fifteen cents. Featured in the show were "New Songs, Dances, Negro Farces, Contortion and Acrobatic Feats, Burlesques, Pantomimes, Dramas, Music." At the top of the broadside in bold black letters appeared "$500 REWARD! BOYLOST." "MISSING," the account read, "from about the third of next month, 1870, a tall complexioned young man, about five feet six inches of age; hight thirty-seven years; had on when last seen a pair of swallow tailed sealskin trowsers, with sausage stripes, fashionable mutton chop waistcoat, with cast-iron trimmings, double-barrelled frock coat, with stripe collar and tobacco lining: watertight canvas boots, with patent leather tops, laced up the side: is deaf and dumb of one eye and hard of hearing with the other; is slightly pockmarked at the back of his head, stoops upright when he walks crooked; has a slight impediment in his look, and wears a Grecian bend on his upper lip; whiskers cut off short inside; was carrying an empty carpet box in each hand, and a wooden leg in the other, containing screw steamers, railway tunnels, and blacking; was born before his young brother, his Mother being present on the occasion."

When measured on a nanometer scale, my discoveries don't amount to much. But when measured by inches, feet, and yards, my research rises square rigged, enabling me to tack unperturbed like a frigate bird high above any archipelago. Who wouldn't want to know that the lost boy had a pocket book in his possession "containing a Ten-Dollar Gold Piece, One Silver Watch, Two Large Hams, One Barrel of Flour, One Load of Wood, One Rocking Chair, 2 Setts of Glassware, 10 Setts Cups and Saucers, 4 Dozen China Plates, 1 Washtub, 1 Stove, 1 Pig, and 50 other beautiful presents"? "Selections" from the list, the broadside informed passersby, would be given away during the troupe's performance at the "Public Hall."

I have long planned the arbitrary course of my studies. Occasionally, however, my doings seem indulgent. The Office of Undergraduate Research, a flyer explained, provided "research-related opportunities . . . to students interested in engaging in independent or collaborative research with faculty members and research professionals." In May I reversed course and, sailing with the institutional wind, decided to form a research team. The team differed slightly from that envisioned by OUR, as the Office of Undergraduate Research calls itself, because the student's collaboration consisted only of urging me to view the SpongeBob Square-Pants thermometer on sale at Walmart.

Accordingly one morning Vicki and I drove to Willimantic. To prepare for roaming Walmart, we stopped at Bagel One, and I munched a crazy bagel, that is, one bristly with onions and an assortment of seeds, slathered with butter not cream cheese, however, as I wanted to remain alert with blood coursing through my head rather than collecting in my lower regions. Incidentally only great experience in cafés and diners has enabled me to calculate the optimum number of calories suitable for research. Determining catalytic calories from fat was especially difficult. A smidgen too much fat induces sleep not thought.

Research trips always turn up the unexpected. After eating our bagels, Vicki and I walked across a parking lot to All Pets Club. "Not to be missed," Vicki said. She was right. Like lavish icons decorating canticles in medieval Psalters, a menagerie swam illuminated across the beginning of my work: orange and white clarkii clowns, $29.99 each; yellow tangs, two for $39.99; tiger barbs; neon tetras flashing red and blue; angelfish; marble and black mollies; fancy guppies at $3.99 a pair; and for $4.99 each, albino channel cats, these last sweeping traces of gluttonous extravagance from the bottoms of aquariums. While Russian tortoises were on sale for $103.99, six dollars knocked off the regular price, ferrets and guinea pigs rumpused through newspapers shredded in their cages. "Undergraduate researchers," Vicki said. "Not quite those imagined by OUR," I answered. The club was so seductive that purpose almost slipped out of mind. To recapture the informed practicality of our trip, we forced ourselves to leave and drove half a mile to Sears, where I purchased two air filters for my lawnmower. The transition from Sears to Walmart was smooth—the physical distance a hundred yards, the intellectual distance almost nonexistent.

Researchers often spend hours lost amid the data of test tube and survey. For my part I strode intuitively to the pharmacy section of Walmart and immediately discovered the SpongeBob thermometer. Bob was a thermometer for all orifices, suitable for oral, underarm, and rectal use. Priced at $9.38 and six inches tall, Bob was digital, supplying a "temperature read–out" only nine seconds after insertion. His square yellow head sat atop a tapering yellow triangle. Bob's eyes were sea blue. His eyebrows curved upward in excitement. A smile spread across his face, revealing two gleaming buck teeth. Beneath his chin glowed a small red tie; under it stretched a narrow white shirt and a black belt. At the conclusion of "temperature taking," the thermometer played the SpongeBob SquarePants theme music. "Did you know . . . ?" a question on the packaging started to ask but interrupted itself, supplying the answer before finishing the sentence, "The Velcro mat outside SpongeBob's front door says 'ahoy.'"

Research is never ending; one observation invariably leads to another. As I studied Bob, I heard a man in the next aisle ask where he could find Imodium A-D. I walked to the end of my aisle and peered around the corner. The man looked hale, but as gastroenterologists often say, appearances can deceive. For her part Vicki gave Bob short shrift, proving herself to be a fellow traveler, one with capitalist not communist leanings, however. While I pondered an elegant way of taking my temperature, she decamped, reappearing with $31.07 of purchases: sixty caplets of Equate Dairy Digestive Supplement, two pounds of Miracle-Gro Liquid All Purpose Plant Food, 3.74 pounds of bananas, a bag of California mandarins, two doormats, and a Snickers bar. Excluding gas, the research trip cost $53.52, $7.10 being expenses at Bagel One and $15.35 the price of the air filters—not enough for me to undergo the ordeal of filling out paperwork necessary to recoup the money from the University Research Foundation.

As the principal investigator of my days, or P.I. as the National Science Foundation labels grant recipients, I've accumulated untold observations. I have not hammered any of this data, however, into a theory. In fact as people age beyond optimism so I have aged beyond the theoretical, believing that theories smack of the Holy Ghost, their dry bones animated by gusts of poppycock and wishful thinking. Still, life is more various than fiction, and if a person does not study his surroundings, existence will slip past and his life will be a blank tablet unmarked by observation and love. People know ordinary doings intrigue me, and they send me anecdotes. "Thought this morning's typical conversation would interest you," Jared wrote. Jared worked as a cashier at Ocean State Job Lot. "Hello," Jared said to a customer, "would you like to donate to the local food bank?" "No," the customer replied, "why don't they donate to me?" "This item doesn't seem to want to scan," Jared continued scrutinizing an object in the costumer's basket. "It won't scan, then it must be free," the man replied. "Your total comes to $19.23," Jared said after the item scanned. "Nineteen twenty-three? That was a good year," the man responded, picking up his bag. "Hello," Jared said to the next person in line, "would you like to donate to the local food bank?"

"What's significant about that?" Vicki asked after I repeated Jared's conversation to her. "I'm not sure," I said, then quoted an epitaph I recently saw in a graveyard, a statement, I added, that I'd like carved on my tombstone. "While he lived he was alive." The truth may be that I am not so much researcher as hunter-gatherer, almost every day setting out on a localized safari, returning home with bags of words, the game alive and sometimes kicking, but always treated gently, never carved or seasoned into importance. Last month my friend George described an Episcopal minister who was so parsimonious he walked only on grass and avoided sidewalks in order to extend the life of the outsoles of his shoes. One day a bishop visited the minister in the rectory. After a cup of tea, the bishop used the lavatory, noticing the bathtub in the room was full of water. On returning to the parlor, the bishop mentioned the water, thinking a pipe might be leaking and wondering if the tub should be drained. "Oh, no, the water has been there just four days," the minister replied. "I don't change the water until a week has passed. One doesn't want to live extravagantly and set a bad example for parishioners."

I don't anticipate my studies leading to "meaningful" results. Nevertheless surprise enlivens the passing parade. In June I drove to Tennessee and taught for six weeks in the Sewanee School of Letters. Research has become habitual, and during the trip I kept a pencil and notebook handy, jotting down, for example, tonal differences between Virginia and Tennessee. The first and last prose I noticed in Virginia appeared above sinks in the men's bathrooms at rest stops. Pasted on all the mirrors was a sticker asking, "ARE YOU VIRGINIA'S NEXT TRAFFIC FATALITY?," the letters a blare of scarlet. Soon after I crossed into Tennessee, a billboard loomed beside the road, advertising "GUNRUNNERS." "BUY-SELL-TRADE," the sign urged, appealing to drivers anxious to disarm before crossing into Virginia and to those eager to load up before proceeding deeper into East Tennessee—guns being contraceptives preventing their bearers from becoming 187s, the California penal code section for murder—a numerical tidbit I picked up on my travels, not information learned in the controlled work space of a research center. For the index of the next revision of the lab manual a DB is, by the by, a Dead Body while a DRT is a Dead Right There.

While I was in Tennessee, guns were on minds as well as in cars. Newspapers were mailboxes crammed with letters from sots arguing the Constitution allowed them to carry their "best friends" into bars. Of course shortsighted stuffed shirts wrote letters urging curtailing the rights of gun owners, soporifically arguing that "drunks and guns don't mix." "If I were in the Tennessee legislature," my friend Innis said, "I'd sponsor a bill requiring bars to stock pistols and forcing them to hand one to every souse who staggered through the door. To insure the well-being of the community, I'd stipulate that the guns lacked safeties, had hair triggers, and were fully loaded with a bullet chambered. Then when the peckerwoods got shitfaced they would exterminate each other, in the process improving evolution, at least locally, though, having heard only of Fatuous Design, families would not realize the benefits bestowed on society by the cropping of relatives."

I collected a hoard of sentences in Tennessee. Simplification precipitates most explanations. When wedged, period to capital letter, together in paragraphs, the sentences I gather never dice experience into meaning. Diners wrote on the walls of Holy Smokes Barbeque in Monteagle, Tennessee, probably not a strategy that the Food Marketing Policy Center at Connecticut has ever recommended to increase patronage. Nevertheless the restaurant and its walls were as busy as cuneiform tablets. Many statements were religious, "In His presence there is FREEDOM" and "Jesus is awesome" being typical. Several offered bad advice, "Follow your dreams and live with your heart," for example. While Tolkein's "All who wander are not lost" was appealingly rational, "What do you call a male lady bug?" was seductively quirky. Amid clutter often lurks the startling. Buried under a fist of letters scratching over a crook in a wall were six words, "War is murder set to music."

At Sewanee I learned that south of Tennessee this is the "Year of Alabama Small Towns." Moreover the motto on the state's license plate has recently been changed from the anatomical "Heart of Dixie" to the bonbonish "Sweet Home Alabama." Officialdom imposed both slogans. In Tennessee sloganeering arises from the citizenry and as a result is more literary. At the conclusion of the School of Letters I decided to visit Mother and Father, so I returned to Connecticut by way of Carthage. Instead of driving east then west on interstates, I took the old state road north from Manchester, passing through Woodbury and Liberty. The road twisted through valleys, following riverbeds, bottom lands above the banks clabbered with green, the cuts for the road itself frothy with kudzu. In past years the sides of gray lowland barns served as advertising columns, "See Rock City" being almost ubiquitous. Advertising was still present, but it was less secular and more celestial, two examples being "Courage is fear that has said its prayers" and "God wants full custody not weekend visits."

In Carthage I had a picnic with Mother and Father in the Mountain Cemetery. I ate a peanut butter and jelly sandwich and drank a Pepsi-Cola. I did all the talking, and the day was hot, indeed uncomfortable, at a hundred degrees. But Mother and Father didn't seem to mind. I think they liked the flowers I bought at Sheila's Florist on Main Street, a bouquet of blue flag, goldenrod, pink roses, lady ferns, and red carnations wrapped in shiny green paper, around the middle a bow made from purple mesh. I'm not sure that they admired the planter's hat that Mrs. Carver gave me after I dropped by the Sanderson Funeral Home. I like the hat, however, and have worn it on several research trips in Storrs. The band around the crown is claret; sewn on it in silver thread is the name *Sanderson*. Rising above the name is a silver disk, a capital *S* and the date 1904 flickering in the middle like sunspots.

For the true scholar, every day, as OUR put it, offers "research-related opportunities." After the picnic I drove to Hilltop to visit Houston McGinness. Houston is one of the last people in Carthage who knew my family, and whenever I'm in town, I see him. I rapped loudly on his door. Houston is ninety-two years old, and when he didn't appear, I suspected he had not heard me. Consequently I drove to the library behind the courthouse and asked the librarian to telephone him. Houston had been in the basement. I returned to his house, and we had a good visit. I learned that among the entertainments brought to Carthage by the "Mighty Haag" circus in 1928 was "Blue Eyes," the first girlie show Houston attended and the first he thought "to come here," adding that "within a few years all the carnivals at county fairs featured girlie shows." To maintain my reputation for integrity and academic objectivity, let me say that I saw my first bare female at a girlie show at the Tennessee State Fair. Complete disclosure forces me to add that despite scrutinizing the performer's nether lands, giving myself a crick in the neck in the process, I was unable to distinguish this from that.

Focus is a rivet, its head and buck tail fastening mind and eye and banishing play from research. In contrast life flourishes amid the loose and the unpredictable. For me research quickens when inattention drifts like a cloud across my lenses and I become a nilder-nalderer. Amid the heady pleasures of the picnic, buying flowers, donning a new hat, and talking to Houston, I ceased dreading the eleven hundred miles that would machine the hours ahead. On the way out of Carthage I stopped at the Smith County Heritage Museum. The museum was new and located in a flat unappealing building that once must have been a warehouse. Initially I drove past the museum, but then whim turned me around. When Trina, the administrative assistant, said she was from Pleasant Shade, adding that it was "a nice place to be buried in," I almost snapped my fingers. The holdings of the museum were as various and appealing as the contents of BOYLOST's pocket book, and I meandered happily about, at home amid a barn of farm machinery—a cream separator, corn planter, sorghum mill, cast-iron wash pot, and corn sheller among other items. I stood behind a pulpit that had supported a hundred years of sermons in the Chestnut Mound Methodist Church. I sat in a pew donated by the Jack Apple Church, also in Chestnut Mound, and wondered how many people had sat on the same boards.

In a corner of the museum was an exhibit devoted to the Civil War. Some twelve hundred Smith Countians, including at least one slave who accompanied his owner, fought for the Confederacy. To the Union, Smith County supplied a "Regiment of Colored Troops" and three hundred white soldiers, most of whom joined the "Tennessee Mounted Cavalry." I wandered about idly until I noticed two framed pieces of paper, nine by six inches, the writing on them swirling and elegant. Both were receipts written and signed in 1863 by my great-grandfather, William B. Pickering, a Union soldier from Ohio and a first lieutenant and adjutant of the Middle Tennessee Cavalry. John Waggoner, a local historian, donated the receipts to the museum after finding them in a book he purchased at a yard sale. When I had trouble following my great-grandfather's handwriting through its loops and swirls, Trina telephoned John, and he came to the museum and helped me decipher the receipts. The first receipt was signed on May 5, 1863 at "Camp near Carthage" and acknowledged receiving a noncommissioned officer's sword, shoulder strap, and plate. "Received," the second receipt read, "at Carthage, Tenn. This 13th day of July 1863 of A. T. Cottrell, Col 24th Inf 6th Reg, East Tennessee Volunteer Inf . . . The Following Ordnance and Ordnance Stores, 1000 / One Thousand / Cartridge elongated cone ball / Cal. 54."

The receipts thrilled me, my excitement tempered by the realization that I'd almost neglected to stop at the museum. "Thank goodness, I'm a putterer," I thought as I left Carthage, turning east onto Interstate 40. On the trip back to Connecticut, I noticed only two statements painted on barns, the first expected and conventional, the second almost a puzzler: "Jesus Savior. I am the Way, the Life, and the Truth" and "As the Tree Falls So It Must Stand." Still the drive seemed easy, the hours I dallied through in Carthage insulating me from the incessant thrum of tires revolving over asphalt. As long as a scholar is seriously committed to piddling and avoids classifying in order to exclude, research will multiply his interests and brighten his hours. The ways to experience life and its many partial truths, and falsehoods, are infinitely various and alluring. Two weeks ago while doing research in the university library, I stumbled across an account of Lenten customs. Near Altare, where the Apennines join the Ligurian Alps, Christians once celebrated Lent, not by narrowing their days and denying pleasures, but by embracing the unexperienced and, often, the ostensibly distasteful. In so doing, their lives expanded wondrously. They came to appreciate neighbors whose manners differed from theirs. They learned that appearance lied. They discovered that pinched, sunken apples were often sweet and that yesterday's drab bud became tomorrow's flower more beautiful than the rainbow. In transforming themselves, they transformed their worlds. Research, at least research with my kind of shadowy focus, does the same.

Resort

Dreaming begins in late fall and stretches through winter. In November I dreamed that I was raking leaves and woke up musty with perspiration, blankets scraped into a pile. I went downstairs to the kitchen, drank a glass of orange juice, and for twenty minutes stared at the linoleum before returning to bed to be smothered by leaves again. In December snow fell, and I dreamed I was shoveling the drive. I pitched my blankets to the side of the bed and sat up, my back throbbing and my forehead wet and icy. For her part Vicki became a mariner riding the storm-tossed mattress, occasionally waking and shouting, "Hearty, har, har, har, matey," ending with a raspy "argh," the sound the cry of a landlubber's being eviscerated by a rusty cutlass.

When working dreams fill the night, lassitude infects the day. Often surprises billow through moments, however, pushing one beyond the doldrums. From Australia in December, Barbara Olds sent me a poem from her collection *Boundary Rider*. The title of the poem "Promise" was also the first line.

Promise
when I die
you'll scatter my ashes
at sunset
in the hills
overlooking the Mundi Mundi

where I can watch
wild horses
as they chase
their shadows
across red earth

where a thin dark line
divides land and sky
burnt and blue
reflected
in the steaming air

where
no longer bound
by the gravity of life
the willy willy
will set me free

To be plucked from leaves and snow by a dust devil and spun over the Mundi Mundi flatlands and through the horizon appealed to me. For a moment I imagined red sand and stringy blue skies, kangaroos, whistling kites, and black-faced wood swallows. In dream season, though, the poetic fit does not last long. Two days later I saw "Positive Exposure," an exhibition of photographs of albinos taken by Rick Guidotti in Tanzania. Albinism, a broadside said, affected one out of every four thousand people in Tanzania. Melanoma was epidemic, and the average life span of albinos in Tanzania was thirty years. In the West the life expectancy of people with albinism was the same as that of the general population. Melanomas splotched people posing for Guidotti, spreading in brown webs under the skin like the hyphae of mushrooms. In West Africa the bodies of albinos were considered magical and, if stewed into portions brewed by witch doctors, were thought to bring riches. During the past year the broadside stated, at least twenty-eight, and perhaps as many as sixty, albinos had been murdered and parts of their bodies "hacked off and sold to witch doctors."

Such exposure darkened days, causing the Dickensian jollity associated with December to catch in the throat. Moreover at Christmas the dead seemed more with me that the living. In fact I had more to say to the dead than to the living, and only champagne therapy enabled me to fizz through the demands of affectionate small talk. Behind the weariness of December lay not only dream but the stock-market debacle. Much of my retirement vanished, and I spent many gloomy hours mulling my losses. Of course the gloom was intermittent. My friend Nowell sent me *The Pot Thickens,* a cookbook for which he supplied recipes for ambrosia, pimento-cheese sandwiches, baked-bean casserole, apple pound cake, and "the legendary red dressing from the Monroe, Georgia, VFW." The editor of the book commented on the recipes, his remarks rising like soufflés, light to the funny bone rather than to the palette. Of chicken wings a woman served at her annual Superbowl party, he wrote, "I would even sit through a football game for food like this, and the last time I actually sat through a football game, I was dating the quarterback." He then paused before adding, "Oh, never mind, these things do get away from me."

During dream season many things get away from a person. The day after Christmas the immobilizer on my Volvo got its antenna in a snarl, announced "Start Prevented," and shut the car down, blocking the drive. The next morning the car started, and I drove to East Hartford for repairs. While a mechanic massaged cramps out of the immobilizer, I ate breakfast in a diner. Two women in a booth next to me drank coffee and discussed money. They were frightened they were going to lose their jobs, not that their jobs were particularly good, for both lived in buildings infested with rats and roaches. "I'd like to move, but I don't have any money and can't afford anyplace else," one said. "Me, too," her friend replied, then asked, "And what's going to happen to us if we lose our jobs?" "I don't know," the other woman said, twice repeating the sentence, transforming it into a lament.

"I've had an easy life. What does the retirement matter?" I suddenly thought as I dug into the meal in front of me, a plate overflowing with eggs, sausage, toast, and a rockslide of hash browns. On the way home from the Volvo dealership, I decided that Wall Street was not responsible for my losses. Instead my genes were responsible for Wall Street's losses. The depression of 1893 broke my great-great-grandfather Samuel Pickering, supposedly the wealthiest man in Athens, Ohio. In the depression following 1929, my maternal grandfather lost a fortune. Bankruptcy has plagued every other generation of my family, skipping from the paternal to the maternal side. According to genetic schedule, the Pickering side, I, that is, was "scheduled" to go bust. Genetic engineering being in its infancy, I told Vicki, the deflation of our finances was inevitable. "As goes Pickering, so goes the nation." "That's a pretty piece of reasoning," Vicki said. "Yes, isn't it?" I said, no longer feeling bound by the gravity of life.

Snow had begun to shred the line that "divides land and sky," so I went for a walk in hopes of sensing the season's white drift. A horned lark hunkered on the shoulder of a gravel road. The lark's wings were spread. From a distance the bird looked like a broken nest, flipped, its sides splayed. On seeing me, the bird swam across the snow vainly trying to lift itself off the ground. I scooped the bird up. I held it in my hand and slowly opened my fingers, thinking that once aloft the bird would gather the air under its wings and fly. I was wrong. The bird tumbled bedraggled to the snow. I scooped it up again and, putting into my coat pocket, carried it home. I lined a shoe box with a towel and, after wrapping the lark in a dishcloth, put the bird in the box. Later that afternoon Vicki took the lark outside, hoping the warmth of the kitchen had restored the bird's ability to fly. Again the bird fell to the ground, wings shuttering.

That night Vicki brought a Victorian bird cage down from the attic and put the lark inside. At one end she fashioned a nest using an old blue sweater. At the other she put a jar top filled with water, beside it a smorgasbord of food: a bottle cap containing Skippy Peanut Butter, three kinds of granola, and a mashed blackberry. The next morning the bird was frisky but still "lame." When I walked to the university library, Vicki made a telephone book of calls, eventually locating a bird rehabilitator who agreed to meet me in the parking lot of the Ocean State Job Lot near Manchester, forty minutes away on icy roads. Along with the bird I gave the rehabilitator a hundred dollars for the local Audubon Society. A typical lark weighs 1.1 ounces, making our bird, I told Vicki, worth $91 an ounce. "We are lucky I didn't save a pound of larks," I continued when Vicki started to speak, "that would have cost us $1,456. Thank goodness I did not rescue a mature male wild turkey. They can weigh twenty pounds, and I would have had to donate the rest of my retirement, $29,120."

"In the beginning," the Bible states, "was the word." For me the *word* is not God, the divine animating principle of the universe. Instead words are lesser, tarnished things. At their shaping best, however, they alter and create perception. They can shatter melancholy as sunrise does dark night and, by bringing brightness into days, lighten the passing hours. That night a former student sent me an e-mail. He raised tropical fish. Since the end of the semester, he recounted, he had been trying to place me in one of his tanks. "Although your last name is already a fish, chain Pickering, when it comes to being a fish you would be a clown loach," he wrote. "The clown loach is long-lived and originates in the fast moving waters of Indonesia. It is colorful and brings personality to an aquarium. It is intelligent and is resourceful and will out compete tank mates for food. Loaches can be rambunctious. Sometimes they harass tank mates for fun. The loach has a particular trait of lying on its side and playing dead. If disturbed, it will spring to life and swim like hell. If kept in a clean environment, loaches outlive all their friends. Watch out for their spines, though, because they sting." "That's a first," Vicki said, after reading the e-mail. "I hope it pleases you." "Yes, it does," I said. "Immensely."

Words awaken. As a clown loach I was out of my element in the frozen Northeast. Suddenly I longed for, in Barbara Olds's words, "steaming air." Moreover the recession had "set me free," breaking shackles forged by forty years of saving and investing, and I decided to spend the money left in my retirement account. Neither Vicki nor I had been to Mexico. The next morning I booked a week's holiday at a resort on the Riviera Maya, south of Cancun on the coast about halfway to Playa del Carmen. Ten days later we were in a bus thumping down Route 310, the coastal highway, toward our resort, the Paradisus. The highway ran through a long wrecking yard. Resorts hid behind massive walls, guards at the gates. Shoulders of the road crumbled into the rocky detritus of destruction and construction. Suburbs of broken cars rusted into parts, sinking and slumping, tires deflated and rotting. Transmission towers loomed long legged over the ground like starving predators. An occasional small town catered to the traffic, buildings leaning toward the road, genuflecting. Splotches of mangrove appeared here and there, the plots comatose, waiting for developers to drain them and convert them into cornrows of flats, more stubble than stalk and leaf.

The Paradisus was two kilometers east of the highway and on the beach. Similar to all the resorts I saw along the coast, tall fences topped by rows of barbed wire wrapped the grounds. One morning I ran the road up to the highway. "We can't protect you," an employee of the resort said before I started running. "From what?" I asked. "Alligators," he said, looking sheepish. At the corner of the road and the highway was a "zoo." One day before lunch Vicki and I walked to the zoo. The shoulders of the road were narrow, and the traffic thick, consisting mostly of tourist buses, taxis, cement mixers, and pickup trucks loaded with day laborers. The only alligators we saw were in the zoo. Scores lounged leathery around pools amid the wreckage of trees. Deer wandered a paddock, and wild spider monkeys skittered along branches, begging for handouts. Having lost their habitat to development, the monkeys migrated to the zoo and had gotten fat cadging food from visitors. A yellow-headed parrot named Lorenzo said his name, then laughed. I laughed, and Lorenzo laughed again and again. A red coral snake lay like candy amid leaves, its head and tail gleaming black, orange ringing the latter. In contrast to the tweezered gardens of the resort, the grounds of the zoo were appealingly squirrelly, looking like hair after a night's sleep and before being ploughed by a brush.

The Paradisus was an architectural cocktail: Palladian columns; marble floors; Tahitian thatch roofs; balconied three-story American motel buildings, their walls limestone, pools sweeping around terraces and under bridges smacking of Venice; and finally knick-knack Mayan, water dribbling from the throats of jaguars. A vase of Christmas lilies perfumed the lobby, the fragrance overwhelming everyday cares, making one realize he was on holiday. Arrival at the Paradisus did not immediately make me aware I was away from home, however, at least medicinal home. Near the entrance to the resort a board detailed the schedule of a conference, "Issues and Controversies in Prostate Care, 2009," sponsored by the Prostate Center at Vancouver General Hospital, the University of British Columbia, and the Princess Margaret Hospital University Health Network in Toronto. "I suppose the prostate is such a hot topic doctors cannot meet in Canada," Vicki said.

From the side of the main pool, buildings housing rooms stretched along the beach then curved backward forming a U, the arms of the letter cradling gardens. Grass in the gardens was butch and thick and so soaked with fertilizer and pesticide that it resembled artificial turf. Gardeners manicured the plants, turning nooks into hothouse nails. Plantings themselves were the familiar stock of tropical resorts: hedges of bougainvillea, most sections purple but some red; banana; angel's trumpets; thatch palms; poinciana, its seed pods scabbards hanging from branches warped and black; hibiscus; oleander; sea grape, its leaves sturdy round tablets; and croton, yellow breaking from the midveins and flooding over the shallow green surface of leaves.

The gardens were pretty, but they seemed palls, blankets of flowers atop caskets. The absence of life focused Vicki's and my attention on the air, making us ponder the brew of chemicals we inhaled as we strolled walkways. During the week we saw only two insects in our room, this despite leaving the door to the balcony open much of the day: a tiny black ant and a borer beetle resembling a white-spotted sawyer. Occasionally little geckos skittered under leaves, and once we saw a small garter snake hanging like twine in a shrub, its presence revealed by the boisterous nattering of six hooded orioles. Because insects were scarce, birds were rare, the exceptions being melodious blackbirds and great-tailed grackles, these last whistling, sometimes shrieking from perches atop thatch roofs. Turkey buzzards circled the mangrove swamp behind the resort, and once a magnificent frigate bird sailed along the shoreline, riding the wind, looking like an elegant eyelash.

Beyond the beach, brown pelicans bellied into the water, and royal terns zippered over waves. In front of the resort the beach was dead, having been combed out of bird life. Every day a surf rake stripped away seaweed, pottage for the small foragers of surf and sand. On small sections of the shoreline not raked for tourists, minute life swam through low mounds of seaweed, attracting sanderlings, plovers, sandpipers, and ruddy turnstones. Outside the entrance to the resort, tropical mockingbirds sang and flustered through scrub; a clay-colored robin sat in an acacia while a white egret stood motionless in a muddy backsplash. Inland, ocellated turkeys strode through bush, and atop Nohuc Mul pyramid at Coba, a redstart bustled through vines. In summer redstarts hunt insects in the brush bordering the meadow outside the kitchen of Four Winds, our house in Nova Scotia. Seeing a redstart atop Nohuc Mul domesticated the exotic, something that both appealed and didn't appeal to me.

Our room was not, as the resort phrased it, a "Royal Service" room. Instead of east toward the ocean, the balcony faced west and inland, immediately overlooking a tennis court beyond which stretched a mangrove swamp. The room itself was clean and comfortable. Unfortunately workmen were refurbishing other rooms on the stairwell, plastering and painting, with the result that the room often reeked of varnish. The varnish seeped under the door and, at times, seemed to blow through the air-conditioning duct, the result of this last being that we rarely turned on the air conditioning. Instead we left the door to the balcony open, not always, of course, because the smell of pesticide was sometimes overpowering.

Although my sinuses occasionally throbbed, the air did not bother us much because we spent little time in the room. Cruises are floating resorts, and resorts are beached cruises. After dinner, for example, the Paradisus put on a floor show, this featuring dancers, much as shows do on cruises, but involving more pelvic movement than would be comfortable amid the pitch of the ocean. Meals become events on vacations, and the Paradisus had a menu of restaurants: Mediterranean, Japanese, Mexican, French, a steak house, and the Market Place, a buffet. Vicki and I tried all the restaurants except the steak house, diners there appearing to be Americans of the southwestern species, full figured and big buckled. Fare at the restaurants was good, one of the courses always tasty. In contrast desserts were mediocre, not confections a jogger like me should eat in any case. We ate three dinners in L'Hermitage, the French restaurant, all our dinners after eight o'clock. Furnishings of L'Hermitage were more formal than those in other restaurants, imposing civility both on meals and on people who ate in L'Hermitage. The dinner I most enjoyed consisted of snails, followed by mushroom soup, and a fillet, this last something I could have eaten in the steak house. Although cooked exactly the same as for L'Hermitage, the fillet would not have tasted as good in the steak house, the informal seasonings of place and people "gristling" the meat.

At breakfast and lunch, this last if we were at the resort, we ate at the Market Place. The Market Place served the best food at Paradisus. The variety proffered at a buffet is dangerously seductive. Before dinner, people determine to eat modestly, saying they'll sample only a few dishes. Alas samples soon transform diners into mound builders, the trick being to pound the samples into a massive arch dam, its bedrock strong enough to withstand the pressure exerted by thousands of calories. I ate the same breakfast every morning, a packet of All-Bran, over which I dumped a sliced banana, almonds, raisins, two tablespoons of coconut parings, and two small containers of fat-free peach yogurt. At lunch I grazed the green makings of salads after which I felt so virtuous that I treated myself to a bowl of chocolate ice cream swimming in chocolate sauce and topped off with walnuts and knuckles of coconut.

With dinners Vicki and I drank the house red wine, a Montevino. Sometimes the wine was smooth; other times it smacked of vinaigrette. We are not wine bibbers, and never did alcohol turn conversation fuzzy. Before dinner we went to El Mirador, the lobby bar, a huge room with a high thatched ceiling, sides open to the night, and sofas and chairs in comfortable clumps. I know little about mixed drinks, so we sipped soda-pop conglomerations, daiquiris and margaritas, though once I wolfed down a thimble of tequila. We also munched peanuts, something we liked because the bartender drizzled lime juice over them. In the bar we studied people, a dandy pastime when one is away from home, the activity provoking a reassuring dose of snobbery.

Many men talked loudly and looked seedy, like wrinkled college boys returning to school for reunions and determined to recapture the splendor of crass old times. On the van that delivered us from the airport in Cancun to the resort, a man sitting on the seat behind us said he couldn't wait to have an initial hangover, "the first of four," he said. Guests at the resort were palettes of tattoos. On the back of a large woman, a well-fed python twisted through a jungle of philodendron. The resort catered to families, and squadrons of minute children marched through the lobby bar. Many of the children kept cavorting hours and were still roaming at 10:30 when Vicki and I returned to our room. When our children were small, we tucked them into bed before 8:00, and we speculated about parents who unleashed their children, letting them roam the dark hours while they themselves drank away evenings. "Not the sort of people with whom I'd share a bowl of peanuts," I said. "Certainly not," Vicki answered.

Nationalities were distinct: Germans in shorts, the French thin, the Spanish tacky, rouged and ruffled, and Americans bulbous and belly sprung, husbands and wives metaphorically guilty of bigamy, their mates larger than sideboards. Unlike other vacationers, a goodly, perhaps godly, number of Americans prayed before bulldozing through meals. No matter their nationalities, however, tourists were distinct from the Mexicans who worked at Paradisus, most of the former wearing glasses, none of the latter. Ignorance often splattered moments. On a bus traveling to Playa del Carmen, a nearby town, a man spoke to boys sitting across the aisle from him, volunteering that he lived in Omaha and asking where they were from. On their answering Canada and specifying Vancouver, he said, "Oh, yeah, that's near Detroit. Isn't it?" When the boys said Vancouver wasn't close to Detroit, he said, "I thought I might have gotten it wrong. You live just across from New York border, don't you, near one of those lakes?"

Our first night at the resort was clear, the only such night we enjoyed as the weather darkened late the next afternoon. During the middle of week rain fell in leaden sheets. The moon was full that first night, however, and Vicki and I spooned about watching yellow float like a mist across the sky, then moonlight polish the lips of waves into rungs, forming silver ladders. At the resort guests could participate in several activities. Although the next morning was overcast, Vicki and I signed up to snorkel, once that afternoon and again the following morning. We were lucky. During the rest of our vacation the wind banged, swirling the sea, making snorkeling impossible.

For me reefs are gardens. After a moment's snorkeling I splash into a mood akin to the runner's zone. Time unravels, and my energy mysteriously replenishes itself, almost making me believe I can swim endlessly. On both occasions Vicki and I snorkeled offshore in the National Marine Park within sight of the Paradisus. We swam through veiny lettuce coral, delicate sea fan, staghorn, brain, and boulder star coral. We saw fish by the scores: black groupers, their skins dark bricky mottles; golden brown beaugregories; "zebraed" sergeant majors; permits swiveling above the sand; barracudas; needlefish; French angelfish, yellow edging their scales, glittering like the sides of gold coins; and grunts, first blue striped and second pork fish, rails of yellow running along their bodies. Green sea turtles rowed slowly across the sea floor. Large green moray eels poked their heads out of coral snuggeries, and schoolfish snappers wavered in the current like kelp. The most beautiful fish I saw were blue tangs. Clouds darkened their blue skins turning them purple, "the old-fashioned iris of the Caribbean, almost as appealing as the iris grown by Grandma Pickering," I told Vicki.

Cruise companies pad their take by scheduling excursions whenever boats dock. When I lectured on a cruise, Vicki and I did not book excursions, preferring the cheaper and frequently the more entertaining thing of rambling on our own. The Paradisus was comparatively isolated. Shills touted traveling to Cancun and visiting malls, offering free transportation and a complimentary massage. Shopping for presents is part of the vacation experience, especially for adults who have aged beyond the rough and tumble of real adventuring. Still Vicki and I did not travel to Mexico in order to be hauled off to malls. In two comparatively dry afternoons we took buses to Playa del Carmen and roamed Fifth Avenue, the city's tourist strip, the street a long, bright, and alluring food court and glitzy flea market.

One could perk up a stroll along Fifth Avenue by getting a massage. Afterward he could dandify his appearance and have his hair braided. If braiding made him or, perhaps in this instance, her appear silly, too young for tattered age, she could change her look by buying a serape and a shirt or blouse decorated with rows of embroidered flowers. If the braids became unbearably irksome, a person could hide them under a mask, the sort worn by villains in professional wrestling, perhaps one with blue horns or with gold fangs. Cradling a puppet would also divert attention from one's head, particularly a Day of the Dead puppet, a grinning skeleton with jangly knees, just right for skipping through graveyards and bounding over tombstones. If the effort to shed attention drained strength, a person could stoke up by buying banana chips and half a roasted chicken from street vendors, washing the bird down with a mango smoothie, then topping the whole off with a "death by chocolate" gelato as Vicki and I did, Vicki afterward supplementing the snack by visiting a grocery where she purchased potato chips cooked in Mexico, "munchies for the return flight to Hartford," she said, sealing the bag after handing me a handful.

The blare of hawking and hustling was exhausting and exhilarating. Vacationers strode by in gangs speaking a United Nations of languages. Touts tried to lure us into shops and restaurants. Some wore costumes and were dressed as gorillas or wild Indians. Small bands paraded in front of cafés, the members stroking guitars and occasionally shaking mariachis, all the while looking doleful. Tourist police strolled in pairs, their strides slow and easy like those of tired farmers. For respite Vicki and I wandered down Constitution to the beach. Later in the dark we watched ferries blinking ways to and from Cozumel. We went into Capilla de Nuestra Señora, a chapel near the south end of Fifth Avenue. The interior was white with lilies. Along the wall light bulbs flickered behind shades made from conch shells. For a while we left the markets to search for a lavatory, eventually finding one behind a bank on the second floor of a building on Tenth Avenue.

The clamor of buying was seductive, and we explored a score of trinket shops. Jewelry stores glittered although the silver that shined was not necessarily as pure as owners claimed. Still Vicki fondled earrings and necklaces. For my part a small silver jaguar caught my eye. The crush of shops, though, sapped enthusiasm, and we hesitated at the cash register, thinking we could find another shop that sold the same goods at cheaper prices. Stores that sold ceramics were alluringly colorful. One could purchase not only table settings decorated with vegetable and flower gardens, red and green peppers, sun roses and calla lilies, avocados and agave, but also a zoo of creatures: rainbowed macaws, angelfish, and lizards with green heads, blue bodies, and red and yellow tails.

For the tourist who brought an empty suitcase with him to Mexico, a warehouse of ceramic sinks was available, all fantastically painted: among others, green fruits sliced in half revealing fountains of orange seeds; yellow fish with red fins blowing blue bubbles; scarlet airplane propellers attached to golden door handles; spatula-shaped buds, red buttons cinching calyxes and corollas down tightly, preventing the flowers from opening out of season and blowing; and swollen yellow dogwood blossoms clearly plagued by both elephantiasis and jaundice. Most designs were kaleidoscopic, potentially dizzying to shavers, almost certain to swirl focus, causing razors to wobble and, instead of trimming chins, felling jugulars. Appealing to the sybarite, humidors of Cuban cigars and distilleries of tequila lined the walls of shops. "Why don't you live it up and buy a cigar?" Vicki said. The last cigar I smoked was in 1965 after a boat club dinner in Cambridge, England. It and the brandy I swilled afterward to scrape away the bitumen deposited by the smoke corroded my esophagus almost causing a fatal rupture. "Maybe," I said, "but first let's see if we can find you some earrings." Vicki shops slowly, and by the time she settled on a pair of earrings, the time had come to return to our bus stop and the cigar was forgotten.

In snowy Connecticut, Vicki and I imagined relaxing in Mexico, spending lazy unorganized hours, ambling the shore and dozing under beach umbrellas. Instead downpours swept us into activity and drove us from the Paradisus. The cells of travel agents pocked a walkway leading to El Mirador. To escape the rain and its consort, boredom, I booked two eight-hour excursions hoping that away from the coast days might be drier. I mulled renting a car but decided that driving through gully washers in Mexico would turn the vacation into an ordeal. "And probably give you shingles, if not kill us," Vicki said. Both excursions were to Mayan ruins, first Chichen Itza, then Coba. Travel momentarily educates. At the least travel forces a person to realize that his knowledge of the world is partial, something forgotten once the traveler returns home and snuggles down amid the familiar.

A bus fetched us before eight in the morning. On the bus in addition to tourists were the driver, a guide, a supervisor, and a waiter who greeted us with coffee. After we visited Chichen Itza, the waiter dispensed bottles of Corona beer. Few fellow tourists stood out. Across the aisle from us sat a mother, her teenage daughter, and the daughter's girlfriend. The girls slept through the long comings and goings while the mother silently munched candy. Two seats up a stolid Polish family guzzled beer, their expressions changing only when an aged woman suffering from digestive difficulties used the lavatory under a side staircase, the noises she made causing the family to snort gleefully.

The bus drove to Cancun, then turned west, leaving the state of Quintana Roo and taking a toll road into Yucatan. The landscape was scrubby. Soil atop the limestone was thin, and trees were small, the largest kapok trunks tall, thin tapered bottles, the bark fleshly, gray and smooth. Vines roiled into tangles, and woody daisylike flowers bloomed yellow along the shoulders of the road. Tour companies season trips with variety and break days into "eye bites," assuming that tourists have limited spans of interest and are incapable of concentration, even at sights as startling as Mayan ruins. The bus stopped first at a souvenir cooperative. Goods for sale were the same as those in Playa del Carmen. Because Indians sold the goods, however, they seemed more authentic. Later the tour stopped at a cenote where passengers could swim. Cenotes are sinkholes that form in limestone and fill with water. Some are open and look like rounded, roughly thrown pots, while others are practically closed, a small opening leading underground. Vicki and I were the only passengers who swam. Cold rain was falling, and steps down to the pool were slippery as fungus. Vines hung down in falls from the open mouth of the cenote, and from the limestone walls ferns flared up in green sconces. Other buses stopped at the same cenote, and while paddling about in the water, I met a soldier who had commanded Canadian troops in Afghanistan. "Oh, hell," I said. "Maybe we can hope," he said. "Maybe," I said, adding, "have a good vacation." "You, too," he said.

On our second excursion Vicki and I traveled in a small van with eight other tourists to Coba. The company advertised the day as a "Maya Encounter" with "Off Track Adventures." On the trip we swam in another cenote, the pool of which was more difficult to reach as we twisted through a thin, broad opening, known as "the frog's mouth" then followed a wooden staircase downward, clinging to a railing. Sheets of stalactites hung from the walls of the sink, some rippled as if they were blowing in a wind. Stalagmites rose from shelves of limestone above the water, one appearing hooded, looking like a friar. The water was green and warm, and edges of the sink curved outward into dark scoops, titillating me as I imagined an underground river sucking me out of sight. This tour was especially fragmented. Early in the morning the rain stopped, and although the adventures were fun, I was eager to explore Coba. In any case we rappelled into what had once been a limestone cave, its roof having collapsed long ago, the bottom gone not to water but to trees and shrubs. After hiking up and out, we rode a zip line across the open mouth of the sinkhole, the zipping and rappelling new experiences for both Vicki and me. Later we canoed across a lonesome lagoon and walked for a short distance through a low, damp forest.

On the second excursion we ate lunch in a Mayan village, outdoors in a small wooden pavilion covered by a raised thatch roof. The food was good: rice with peas, chicken legs in a stew pot brimming with red sauce, taquitos, black beans, and for drink hibiscus juice. Across a dirt road four peccaries dozed in a pen; a puppy slept beside a rock; and a ragged dog walked slowly, her nipples hanging down jagged. In comparison to many of the towns through which we drove, the village looked prosperous. More feral dogs than people seemed to populate some towns. Visible outside towns were sprawling dumps, "Temples to the God Plastic," Vicki said, offerings of black garbage bags, clear bottles, and rolls of white and gray sheets strewn about. During the first excursion we ate at a Mexican buffet patronized by tour companies, eight or nine buses in the parking lot when we arrived. While we ate, women wearing beautifully embroidered dresses danced to entertain us. Cultural imperialism is usually vulgar. Although the steps performed by the women were supposedly "native," the women did them while balancing beer bottles on their heads. Some women were better dancers than others, balancing not a beer bottle, but a tray in the middle of which sat a whiskey bottle. At the edge of the tray shot glasses circled the bottle.

"I didn't book this trip to see that," I said to Vicki as we left the restaurant. What we took both trips to see were Mayan ruins. They exceeded imagination and thought, maybe even the possibilities of contemporary thought. For a while at Chichen Itza, we listened to our guide. He was good, but the palaver of even the best guide can be found in a book, so we roamed, marveling at the Castle of Kukulkan, the ball court, the observatory, the church, and sundry temples, those of the jaguars, warriors, and carved panels, among others. In part we roamed to escape words that inevitably narrow and shackle one to the present. The limestone buildings rose so tarnished and pitted from the jungle that we could not see them clearly and, as a result, half-created them in imagination. We studied carved stone panels and picked out flowers, skulls, rattlesnakes, and birds.

Along both sides of the path leading from the ossuary to the Red House, villagers set up tables and sold crafts. Americans don't inhabit cultural dreamtimes rich with mythic and ancestral stories. Americans are mobile. Family memories are usually short and often are not bound to place. As a result Americans purchase objects. Not only can objects mark the course of a life, but also the sight of them quickens recollection. I did not care if Playa del Carmen slipped loosely from mind like grass clippings in a breeze. But I wanted something that would make me remember Mayan ruins. At Chichen Itza women wandered about selling handkerchiefs embroidered with flowers. Vicki bought six handkerchiefs, then two saucers, both different from anything she saw in Playa del Carmen. For my part I studied woodcrafts. Most of the carvings were similar and almost looked like machines had cut them. For a while I watched a man carving the head of a jaguar. Such heads were commonplace, however, and I did not buy the head. Displayed near the ossuary, however, was a row of panels carved from Spanish cedar. One panel was different from the others. The panel was twenty-eight-inches tall and ten wide and had just been stained, most of the carving brown but some parts dark cream. A Mayan king knelt in the middle of the panel. Atop his headdress a rattlesnake rolled through two coils, jaws spread, fangs sharp, tail draped behind, the rattles almost beads on the king's headdress. In his hand the king held a representation of a god. On the panel also appeared three jaguars and the heads of three men, their hair bound, looking like sheaves of grain. Vicki saw me studying the panel. "Look at that snake," she said, adding, "You have to buy it." I hesitated. "Maybe I will see something I like better at Coba," I said. "You won't," Vicki said, opening her purse and handing me money. "Now go bargain."

Vicki was right. At Coba souvenirs were snakeless. Moreover the tour company allocated only ninety minutes to Coba, filling the day with rappelling and canoeing. Little restoration had been done at Coba, and ruins loomed mysterious beyond paths, the jungle a wiry green canopy growing over and through them. Vicki and I learned from visiting Chichen Itza. After buying juice freshly squeezed from grapefruits and oranges, we abandoned our group and wandered the exposed ruins on our own, climbing them as we were not allowed to do at Chichen Itza. Nohuc Mul pyramid, the most famous sight at Coba, was slightly over a mile from the entrance to the ruins. We rented bicycles, the first time Vicki had been on a bicycle since childhood, and raced each other along a path to the pyramid. Nohuc Mul was 42 meters and 120 steps high, though Vicki counted only 118. I don't know why people climb. Maybe they do so to say, if only to themselves, that they climbed. In any case Vicki and I climbed Nohuc Mul. At the top we agreed that the government would soon stop tourists from climbing Nohuc Mul. "But we can say that we climbed it," Vicki said. "You bet," I said. Below the pyramid the land spread skirted in trees, ruins rising in green knots, lakes open like eyes.

We are now back in Connecticut. Bracelets of ice wrap limbs, and snow is thick over the ground. We had a fine time in Mexico. The panel leans against a wall in my study close to a jarrah burl I picked up in Western Australia. A fortnight ago I drove to Cabelas, a new store in East Hartford specializing in hunting equipment, Vicki having said, "Seeing won't make you a believer." In the middle of the store an artificial mountain rose to the ceiling. Perched on it was a zoo of stuffed animals. Hanging like molding on walls were animal heads and a Caribbean of fish. On a balcony stood an elephant, a sable antelope, a rhinoceros, and an eland among an Africa of other four legged creatures. The gun department could have outfitted a regiment. In the North Fork Shooting Gallery, children fired laser guns at Bambi and his mother and father as they loped across the screens of "Big Buck Hunter" and "Big Buck Safari." Most of the children were so small that their fathers supported the guns for them and told them when to shoot, some yelling if their offspring reacted slowly. Outside the gallery a recording tried to attract little gunners saying, "I think these kids would rather go into the laser shooting gallery and give it their best shot." Sometimes the voice declared, "And you thought you'd seen everything." I agreed with the voice. I thought the sight of parents steadying guns for their kids was, I said to Vicki, "damn near the end of everything." I spoke too soon. Vicki and I ate lunch in the store, ordering buffalo burgers. A table near us was empty. Before we left, two men sat down. They were neo-Nazis, the first and, I hope, the last I ever see. They wore black shoes and socks, black trousers, and black sweatshirts, on the chest of which appeared two jagged bolts of white lightning, the insignia of the SS.

"The store is a nightmare," I said to Vicki as we left. My dreams, though, are better than they were before Vicki and I went to Mexico. Last week I dreamed that a monstrous blue horse was chasing me through the woods behind our house. When the horse got within trampling distance, I pulled a pistol out of my belt and shot him, the sound of the gun not disturbing my sleep. During the day I reckoned I bought the pistol at Cabelas, though I can't be positive about that. In any case school has started, and three nights ago I dreamed I lost a student's paper. I almost woke up and started searching for the paper. Before I began rooting under the covers, I thought for moment. "In forty years in the classroom I've never lost a student paper, so this must be a dream," I concluded, "and I'm not going to wake up." Yesterday Vicki and I went to the book sale at the local library. I looked at a book entitled *The Colony of Unrequited Dreams* but didn't purchase it, thinking the characters probably too frustrated to be appealing. I did discover a gem, though, *Varicose Veins* written by two doctors, published in 1939, and containing "Fifty Text Illustrations" and "Two Color Plates." Blood vessels depicted on the plates looked like tangles of poison ivy, while many legs were thicker than the trunk of the largest kapok tree I saw in Yucatan. I teach a course in children's literature. When students ask me to define "children's book," I always say, "a book read by a child." Today I passed *Varicose Veins* around the class. In several photographs, people were nude. Before handing the book to students, I stuck fig leaves of pink Post-it notes over the sufferers' nasties. Atop each Post-it, I wrote, "Do not lift. The sight below is unappetizing." I also repeated my definition of a children's book, after which I noted that children found medical books endlessly intriguing. "According to a survey conducted in Mansfield during 1960s," I said, "for four consecutive years more children checked *Varicose Veins* out of the library than any other scientific book." When students looked puzzled, I said, "Hearty, har, har, har, matey." After a pause I ended with a rollicking "argh."

Be of Good Cheer

In 1712 Joseph Addison said cheerfulness was "a *Moral* Habit of the Mind" that turned "the Universe into a kind of Theatre filled with Objects that either raise in us Pleasure, Amusement, or Admiration." Alas scruples cause stage fright and, diminishing the capacity for merriment, lead one to avoid treading the boards of life. Happiness depends upon not being overly concerned about the doings of others or the self. Indeed real cheerfulness may be possible only in eroding age when concerns begin to fall away, this happening despite ailments and flocks of one's friends earning their wings, as an obituary I read last month stated.

Education convinces naive youth that life is real, earnest, and capable of being ordered. Schooling celebrates analysis and implies that problems can be solved. Happily classroom injections eventually lose their toxicity, and unless a person swallows a retarding dose of ambition, he realizes that profundity is a mistake and that about the only thing that can be expected in life is drift. In college I belonged to the Phi Delta Theta fraternity, one of the popular songs of which was "Tell Me Why She Wears His Pin." The title was the first line, after which came, "Tell me why she's strong for him. / Tell me why she is so true. / She told me why; now I'll tell you. / Because he is a Phi Delt bold, / Because he is a knight of old, / Because he wears the Sword and Shield [design of the fraternity pen], / That is the reason she had to yield." "Too simple, not a good explanation," I thought when I recalled the song last week. "But not something that matters," I said aloud, shifting my attention to a sentence in G. K. Chesterton's *Tremendous Trifles,* "Every now and then I have introduced into my essays an element of truth."

In February a reporter sent me a series of questions she hoped I'd answer for an article she was composing on writing. The reporter was young, and the questions smacked of excelsior and platitudinous elevation. She wanted to know who "inspired" me "to become a writer," and "how important" it was to me "to influence the next generation of writers." "No one inspired me," I wrote in response to the first question. "Writing, like marriage, happened." In answer to the second question I replied, "If I thought what I wrote really influenced people, I would glue my pages together." Thirty years ago I would have spaded up the bones of someone who inspired me. I hope that I would not, however, have risen to the bait of thinking my words influential. A year ago I heard a commencement speaker declare, "Everyone loves to be around a leader." No, the sensible do not frequent tanning salons, and few adults enjoy basking in the glow radiating from the foreheads of leaders. Certainly no leader loves to be alone around himself.

The reporter didn't understand that old age is not contemplative. A person is most susceptible to contemplation and melancholy in his early middle years. During this period questions about inspiration and influence raise the spirits, making one think his doings important, and if the deluding effects of education still occasionally throb along an artery, he may consider himself a credit to his schooling, someone who should be active in his college's alumni association. Old age realizes that amid the drift of life only small matters sparkle. The reporter asked me what "literature" I had read recently. Significance hangs like cellulite on the word *literature*. To paraphrase the gospel song, I have laid the burden of literature down, if not by the riverside then by the library door, and analyzing reading intent upon discovering meaning is just one among many things I "ain't gonna" study no more.

The commencement speaker urged students to "approach life with a positive attitude," sensible advice for the young and the tiresomely, perhaps dangerously, hormonal. For my part I have aged beyond attitude as well as meaning, and I read not for inspiration or thought but for glittering shards, sentences and paragraphs that make me smile: for example Richard King's observation in *With Silent Friends,* "Those who strive to make the world better usually die alone" or Charles Colton's noting in *Lacon* that "some reputed saints that have been canonized ought to have been cannonaded, and some reputed sinners that have been cannonaded ought to have been canonized." Occasionally sentences make me chuckle, and I quote them to Vicki at dinner, last week a remark from Robert Lynd's *Essays on Life and Literature,* "It is said that in the end men grow tired of the body, and are glad enough to leave it. Those who do, I fancy, are bolder spirits than I. I am naturally a stay-at-home, and the only home in which I have lived all my life is my body."

Addison said that cheerfulness banished "all anxious Care and Discontent," something difficult to do during these the carpenter ant days of March. Yards are boggy and thatched with branches and twigs. Cold rains chill the sap of expectation. Husbands and wives become dry and prickly, and live around not with each other. Sinuses bloom into throats grittier than roadsides gravelly from the throws of a dozen sandings. Through periwinkle and pachysandra and under the splayed trunks of silverbells, the last oak leaves to fall in December clump together, seeming to pull dirt into them, forming calloused gray mounds. Happily education often fails to stamp youth into socially and grammatically correct behavior, and students keep me cheerful. Carol described a girl she once knew, writing, "She had the personality of a small soap dish." In an essay Chip recounted being voted "Most Respected" during his last year of high school. The vote puzzled Chip. "I did not play team sports, and I preferred Led Zeppelin to Hip Hop," he wrote. "Moreover, I never missed an opportunity to cheat on a test, and I thoroughly enjoyed every chance for plagiarism. I even created a sort of plagiarism solitaire in which the sources I stole from were assigned points on a graduated scale. Obscure sources scored low on the scale, usually within the two hundred to four hundred point range while more recognizable writers like Thoreau could score thousands of points depending on the passage. Plagiarizing *Walden* and getting away with it was easily worth two thousand points." Chip will go far, I thought. I gave him an A, influenced by the graduation speaker's remark, "everyone loves to be around a leader."

Alice cheered me because she had the courage of her learning, and eccentricity. "I rarely watch television, but when I do, I watch reruns, preferably on the History Channel or ESPN Classic," she wrote. "If constancy is assigned the value k, then a rerun on the History Channel deserves a value of k^2. This second-order value is a result of the two unchanging conditions: the channel and the age of the show. Likewise, there is nothing I enjoy more than watching a movie for which I consider myself an understudy. The ability to recite every word of a script, for not just one, but every single character, is something on which I pride myself, but something a fellow movie watcher may deem irritating. This is probably because he is jealous that he hasn't the mental capacity to retain every line as I have."

Will, however, wrote the piece that blew away the doldrums, so delighting and rousing me that I e-mailed Pest Mall, ordering $104.47 worth of carpenter ant killer. Will described matters that irritated him. "I think that women and men are so different that there has to be things that bother a man about a woman and vice versa. One thing that always bothered me about my ex was that she always asked questions that set me up for failure. I don't like to lie, and when my ex would ask me, 'does my butt look big in these pants?' it would drive me crazy especially if her butt did look big in those pants. She has her own eyes, and if she knows her butt is jumping out of the pants in all directions she should not ask her boyfriend for a second opinion. This is mean because he either has to lie or say 'yes, dear, your butt looks big. I wouldn't wear those pants if I was you.'"

Cheerfulness expands the sensibilities, invigorates the affections, and so awakens curiosity that one observes the world about him, relishing and appreciating being itself. Earlier this year I traveled to Chattanooga for the biennial meeting of the Fellowship of Southern Writers. I tossed through the first night, unable to sleep. At 6:00 the next morning I left my room and roamed the streets around my hotel, looking for a place in which to eat breakfast. As I hunched over the counter of the Inside Restaurant, I dreaded the day ahead, the hours seemingly clogged with a talk at a high school, a lunch and meeting, a panel, then a book signing. "I don't have the energy to eat," I thought, as I stared at the menu. But then I heard a waitress speak to the cook. "Bobby," she said. "I've got to go to the bathroom. I'll be right back." "I'm not surprised," Bobby answered. "I know you are not," the waitress answered. "I'm an old lady." "Oh, yes," I thought, "today is going to be a humdinger," and when the waitress returned from the bathroom, I ordered a pot of coffee, two eggs sunny-side up, grits, biscuits, and a slab of country ham broader than Tennessee, just the breakfast for someone eager to relish the hours. When one has a good appetite, the day rarely lets him down. "I've been married five times to three different men," a lively woman told me at the book signing. "That's nothing," a woman standing nearby said, "I've been married eight times to seven different men." "Country ham, optimism if not sunny-side up at least a few times over lightly, and then buttery grits of marriage," I thought. "What a world."

Two weeks ago I spoke at Nicholls State University in Thibodaux, Louisiana. I flew from Hartford to Atlanta, where I switched planes and flew on to New Orleans. Long trips make me gloomy. A blind man sat near me in the waiting area in the Atlanta airport. When a clerk called our flight, he stood and shuffled toward breezeway leading to the plane. On noticing him, the clerk signaled for him to stop, thrusting out her arm, hand raised like a stop sign. When the man continued shuffling forward, the clerk thrust out both arms. "My god," the woman sitting next to me exclaimed, "he's blind. He can't see her hands." "She's blind, too," I said, suddenly looking forward to Louisiana, knowing I wouldn't need the ministrations of a traiteur, or healer, to get me through the days.

I arrived in Louisiana in good spirits with hankerings not only for okra and catfish, shrimp, and rainbows of beans, but also for glimpses of New Orleans: the Ninth Ward and St. Charles Street, boarded-up and rebuilt houses, high-water marks, vacant lots, and a handyman's shop of college students wielding hammers. Over a platter of oysters a woman described her mother's recent trip to France. The mother was so strict a teetotaler that she refused to enter restaurants in which alcohol was served. When the group with which she was traveling ate in such a restaurant, she remained outside, a friend bringing a plate of food out to her.

I stayed in a private home, something that had made me apprehensive before I left Connecticut. The apprehension vanished as soon as I met Becky and Michael LeBlanc, my hosts. Becky raised a tent in the backyard and held a party for me. Tree frogs trumpeted, and a teacher at a Catholic girls' school said that before her students handed in papers, they put on lipstick and kissed the last page, pressing a pair of red lips onto the paper. On the red they wrote "JMJ," an acronym for "Jesus, Mary, Joseph, Pray for Us." At the party I grazed across Becky's brisket, packing a feedlot of shorthorns around my waist.

Bulldozer and scalpel had transformed a cane field near the LeBlancs' house in a wrinkleless doctor's neighborhood. I roamed the area. Azaleas were pink, and mockingbirds slid through the air landing in trees amid symphonies of notes. Yards seemed almost pressed, houses lounging across them in comfortable assurance. Other neighborhoods were not so tweezered. Along 397 and Kraemer Bayou Road, yards often looked like pottery shops, statues of saints and angels as thick on the grass as cypress knees in the nearby bayou. Brightly-colored plastic Easter eggs big as smudge pots turned other yards into hatcheries, the sort found only at the end of rainbows.

Not only does cheerfulness increase one's enjoyment of life, but it reinforces itself, doubling back from enjoyment and quickening gusto. Becky, Michael, and I spent my last evening in Thibodaux wandering the downtown. Streets had been blocked for a celebration of the arts. Local women sold cookbooks. In a parking lot a rock-and-roll band played "Johnny B. Goode." A horde of small children danced to the music of Cajun Toujours, a spotlight stretching the children's shadows into poles, the distortion creating puppets. On the steps of the Lafourche Parish courthouse, the Moss Pickers played country music, the Dobro making "A

Closer Walk with Thee" longingly lonely and blue. Crowds wandered the streets, everybody seeming to have been high school classmates. I bought a beer at Rene's and even strutted through a bar or two of "Mabeline." Stores and shops were open, and I went into La Tea Da, a "party palace" for little girls, a tearoom imported from the outskirts of Wonderland, cups and saucers on small tables, bows on the backs of chairs, the whole flounced and ruffled, dipped into pinks and pastels cloying with artificial sweetener, and, yet, appealing, just the place in which to celebrate an only daughter's fourth birthday.

One afternoon I cruised Bayou Boeuf in an open flat-bottomed boat owned by Zam's Swamp Tours. Small alligators and turtles basked on logs, the latter beans, the former long trowels, scrubbed and shining. Blue herons and great and snowy egrets fished still inlets. The trunks of bald cypress looked like hoofed bedposts. While Spanish moss fluttered from limbs as if teased into smoky thinness, light flared green from leaves, turning the trees' upper branches into burning bushes. Zam's itself occupied a red wooden building, perched on the bank above the bayou and leaning over the water. Near the entrance to the building, a man hawked refrigerator magnets made from scales plucked from gars. He dyed the scales pink. The magnets cost five dollars and looked like daisies, the scales forming circles, one row stuck under the row above like shakes. Parked in a dining room were three motorcycles. "Did you get those motorcycles from preachers?" I asked a woman sitting at a table. "Naw," she said, "around here preachers drive Cadillacs and Lincolns."

Zam's was cluttered, and I hoped it would be as tacky as places I remembered from my childhood, at one of which Mother bought an alligator lamp for my bedside table. The alligator was small, and its body curved like an S, its tail glued to a slab of wood, forming the base of the lamp. At the top of the S, the alligator's jaws were open, crammed in its throat a socket into which to screw a bulb. At first glance the shop seemed promising. Here and there small alligators twisted dusty along shelves, and a bandolier of bullets curved along a wall. Most items for sale, however, were mass produced. I almost bought a rabbit's foot, but I couldn't decide between one dyed scarlet and one purple. I fondled several rubber snakes and picked up a walking stick with an alligator's head at the top, losing interest when I noticed a bar code pasted to the shaft.

In part Zam's was the traditional highway "zoo." Six baby alligators clambered up, then slid down the sides of a bucket. An aquarium housed newly hatched ducklings. A boa lay in a knot in a cage. Nearby a thick rubber snake stretched across the floor of another cage. A sulphur-crested cockatoo clung to a branch in a dark enclosure. A giant snapping turtle lay at the bottom of a cement tank, the turtle's flesh lumpy and greenish, fungus furrowing its shell and the bottom and sides of the tank. Wire cages contained chickens and a warren of rabbits. A heavy chain fence surrounded a large muddy sink. In the sink were turtles and three or four adult alligators, one of them old and massive. When Lloyd, the son of the owner of Zam's, whacked the alligator on the eye with a stick, it opened its mouth and hissed, the inside of the animal's mouth white and soiled, looking like a pillow on which someone who'd basted his head with lard had slept for a month. Occasionally the alligator lunged at the stick, swishing its tail about and throwing up cataracts of brown water. "Oooh," a forty-year-old woman exclaimed, skipping backward. She and her sister wore identical skin-tight black T-shirts, the shirts so small that they pinched the women's arms into dough and gathered under their breasts, forcing their stomachs into waves of spill. Sequins spiraled around the shirts, forming borders surrounding plots of pink letters. I tried to read the shirts, but the words were wrinkled, and only a physician could justify approaching close enough to puzzle out the letters. "One of life's mysteries," I thought.

Of course domesticity is the great font of cheerfulness. Often decades transform wives and husbands into friendly strangers. Happily for me, Vicki is too bossy to become distant. Our kitchen is small and drab. Not having been painted since we bought the house twenty-six years ago, the cabinets are mustardy with mold. Vicki, though, enlivens the kitchen and meals. Stuck to the fronts of cabinets are a score of three-inch squares of pink paper. Scrolling black like ornamental stenciling across the papers in Vicki's handwriting are contracts. "I, Sam Pickering," a contract typically states, "promise that I will not sneak the chocolate ice cream without Vicki's permission." After the word *signed* appears my signature and the date, for this particular contract February 17, 2009. Vicki knows cheerful people smile away a great deal, including their word, and she reinforces her contracts. To the top of a tub of ice cream she invariably sticks another square of paper, this blue. Printed on the square is a command, usually "Hands Off," "Stay Away" or "Steady On, Sam." If I should so forget myself that I forge ahead and open the tub, I will find another paper, this reading "Have You No Shame?" "Providence," Addison wrote, "has imprinted so many Smiles on Nature, that it is impossible for a Mind which is not sunk in more gross and sensual Delights to take a Survey of them without several secret Sensations of Pleasure."

Vicki's notes transform the kitchen and delight me. Do I always abide by the contracts I sign? Well, sometimes I does, as the countryman put it, and sometimes I doesn't, but be assured that when I don't, I chuckle as I spade out ice cream or dig into the tin of cookies I found yesterday buried under place mats in the fourth drawer of the breakfront in the dining room.

Unsettled

Connecticut is the land of steady winters. Spring drizzles cold and willful through late April. As I await the warm blooms of May, I become impatient and dream of Tennessee, redbuds sprinkled across its hillsides and in its cities mockingbirds cavalierly bucking over yards. Still, once the ground thaws and softens in Connecticut, I break from the house and wintry habit and begin to wander. At first I roam the neighborhood. The flowers of red maples blow and splash into grainy brown pools on sidewalks. For a moment weeping cherries lose their trunks and limbs and become lacy pink veils. Forsythia swells into yellow hedges, and for three or four days star magnolias burst into Milky Ways. The blossoms smell like peppermint and, too sweet for the rough edge of spring, soon shatter and tumble bruised to the ground. At the edge of woods, Quaker ladies gather in demure congregations; around foundation holes peri-winkles blink into blue while guineas graze neglected pastures, clacking nervously, their heads often raised, white like the ivory handles of old walking sticks.

In low woods spicebush blooms in motes of greenish yellow, and along vernal streams false hellebore pushes through the soil in sharp spears, then unpeels broad and seamed. After two or three warm days I gather snakes: ring-necks under till rough along the sides of an abandoned gravel pit; black racers dozing near a copse of field birch; hognoses on a sandy waste, flaring their necks, turning their heads into arrows; and in the temporary spring shallows of the beaver pond, northern water snakes weaving arabesques amid knots of tufted sedge. Familiar sights reassure me, but I also wander in hopes, not of seeing anew, but of seeing some-thing new. Rarely am I disappointed. This year I saw my first spotted turtles, six sunning on platforms of moss and twigs in a still, shadowy pool. Of course not all sights please me, a red-tailed hawk dead in scrub, probably shot by a bored deerjacker, and then two days later a deer tick embedded in my side, the flesh around it proud and sore. For thirty years I have roamed Mansfield's fields and woods. I have harvested hundreds of ticks from my clothes and skin, on occasion more than twenty a day. Never before has one escaped my raking eye and attached itself to me. "I wouldn't worry," Vicki said. "The tick probably won't be carrying Lyme disease." "At this time of the year," I said, "all deer ticks carry the Lyme spirochete."

In early spring Vicki sweeps wintry worries out of mind, and we stray from the house, on a Sunday going to the flea market at the Mansfield Drive-In and afterward treating ourselves to the one-dollar hamburger at McDonald's or on a Saturday buying falafel sandwiches from "Mr. Thank-You Thank-You" at Sarah's Pocket and eating them while watching a track meet at the university, this year spending much time watching girls throw the discus and hammer. Vicki and I were not the only people roaming the lip of spring. Every year immediately before final examinations, my friend Josh drops by my office and makes, as he calls them, a "realistic" comment or two. "Most preachers," he said this year, "aren't the ruffians they appear to be on first acquaintance." "Once upon a time," he continued, changing the subject, "I thought that as I aged, homes would shrink, the places that towered over me in childhood becoming dollhouses. I was wrong. Houses have swollen monstrous with three-car garages and cathedral ceilings, the former signs of dreams vanished into materialism, the latter secular naves revealing an absence of belief."

The end of term always brings oddities, most appealing. During the semester I wear loud neckties ostensibly to awaken students but really to dab color onto my drab, work-a-day personality. After examinations Fernando sent me a present, a blue and yellow necktie decorated with busts of Mozart. "When I was at home exercising in the local gym, I found this wonderful tie hung on a hook. I asked around, and no one claimed it. Instead of letting it get thrown out, I took it. I wanted to give it to you. If you choose to wear it, I hope you think of me." I will wear the tie, my first gymnasium tie, and will think of Fernando fondly. Not long after I received Fernando's present, a friend whom I had not seen in forty-five years dropped by the house. He was a criminal attorney, and on leaving, he handed me his card, two by three and a half inches. Printed on the back of the card were exactly 150 words of advice to clients. "My lawyer," the advice began, "has instructed me not to talk to anyone about my case or anything else, and not to answer questions or reply to accusations. On advice of counsel and on the grounds of my rights under the Fifth and Sixth Amendments, I shall talk to no one in absence of counsel"—good advice for anyone except familiar essayists who have long strayed beyond margins into the indiscreet.

"The detection of absurdity in others," E. V. Lucas wrote, was "one of life's most constant alleviations." Lucas was wrong. The absurdity of others is a boring constant. What really delights is detecting absurdity in the self, puncturing seriousness and cooling the hot flashes of failure. Two weeks ago I ran the Nutmeg State Half-Marathon in Washington, Connecticut. I won my age division, males aged sixty to sixty-nine. "Pretty good for a sixty-seven-year-old," I told Vicki later. "Were you the only runner in your division?" Vicki asked. "Yes," I answered, "I finished first and last. All the others runners in my age group were ghosts." I anteloped along well for seven miles, the pace obscuring my age, I thought, until a younger runner drew alongside. He looked at me, paused for a moment then asked, "Are you all right, sir." Alas, the *sir* stripped the prong from my gait. Still I won some prizes. "A medal, I assume," Vicki said. "Not quite that," I answered pulling a plastic sack out of my canvas carryall. The sack contained a PowerBar, a "Berry Blast Fruit Smoothie" with "natural flavor"; six capsules loaded with Hammer "Beat the Heat" endurolytes; a sample-sized tube of Aquaphor Healing Ointment marked "Not for Sale"; two packets of Hammer Gel, apple-cinnamon flavored "Rapid Energy Fuel," each packet containing ninety calories, none from fat; a packet containing one washload of Penguin Sport-Wash, "Completely removes odors"; and a plastic water bottle slightly larger than a can of Coca-Cola, printed on the outside "endureit multisports," the initial *e* and the *it* in the first word red, the other letters gray, at the end of words an exclamation point. "You're the man," Vicki said after I spread the prizes across the kitchen table.

Memory is an optimist. However, escaping the abrading present is more difficult today than in the past. The age has spawned bloggers who generate material spontaneously and who instead of vanishing anony-mously into the muck of the overlooked send me copies of their writings. To them I seem a "brilliant conversationalist" and "amazing speaker" but withal "completely insane." Dreams also confine a person to the present. The night before the race I dreamed I was writing letters of condolence. The letters were so good that I memorized a paragraph and at two o'clock forced myself to wake up and scribble down what I memorized. "I wish words were more adequate than they are," I wrote. "Platitudes don't come as easily to me as they once did. Memories are thin comforters, but they are comforters nonetheless. Memories have a way of rolling time and the dark present backward into recollection and making one smile. I think nothing betters life more than the clutter of years, each year a sort of attic filled with the momentarily forgotten." Yesterday I slotted the paragraph into a letter I wrote to a friend whose husband died suddenly.

Every year I try to steady the disruptions of spring by planning an academic article, one raised on pillars sunk into the deep bedrock of scholarship. In 1938 E. B. White wrote an essay entitled "The Summer Catarrh." In the essay he noted that Daniel Webster began to suffer from catarrh when he was fifty years old. White argued that the ailment changed Webster's life. Although Webster had presidential ambitions, it "became apparent to him that anyone whose runny nose bore a predictable relationship to the Gregorian calendar was not Presidential timber." Moreover the catarrh dulled Webster's fervor, and he joined Henry Clay in the Compromise of 1850, angering many people. White himself suffered from catarrh, and addressing Webster's critics, he wrote, "What could they know of the scourge of an allergic body? Across the long span of years I feel an extraordinary kinship with this aging statesman, this massive victim of pollinosis whose declining days sanctioned the sort of compromise born of local irritation."

Recently I read *The Cockleshell,* a collection of essays written by Robert Lynd and first published in 1933. From 1913 to 1945 Lynd wrote a weekly essay for the *New Statesman.* Lynd was a celebrated essayist, literate and witty, someone whose writings White would have read, indeed probably studied. In "Early English History Explained," Lynd pondered the effects of harvesters upon British history. (Harvesters are red mites known by many names, chiggers among others.) "Why," he wrote, "should the Britons suddenly abandon the Wansdyke [defensive earthworks in England's West Country]? . . . They were a race, as they proved in less insect-ridden parts, who might be defeated but could not be destroyed. They have shown their capacity for surviving where there was scarcely food for a hawk. Yet at one period in history in the neighbourhood of Stonehenge they must have lost their nerve and bolted, leaving a golden plain of cornland untenanted." "Can it be doubted," Lynd continued, "that, having made their plans for defence against enemies whom they could see, they at last fell victims to an invisible enemy—the harvester. . . . The Briton's capacity for suffering from insect bites had reached the breaking point, and he fled like a hare to the fastness of Wales."

After reading Lynd's essay, White, I concluded, had elevated the earthbound mite to winged pollen, transforming Lynd's insecticidal view of history into the medicinal. In my article I did not intend to toss the germy charge of plagiarism onto the page. In an essay on John Milton in his

Literary Studies, Walter Bagehot wrote, "Some poets, musing on the poetry of other men, have unconsciously shaped it into something of their own: the new conception is like the original, it would never probably have existed had not the original existed previously; still it is sufficiently different from the original to be a new thing, not a copy or a plagiarism; it is a creation, though, so to say, a suggested creation."

Moreover, if a reader challenged the term "suggested creation," calling it weasely, I planned to note that White's and Lynd's contemporaries had begun to find military and social explanations for history tiresome, if not shallow. In 1935 Hans Zinsser's *Rats, Lice and History* appeared in which he wrote, "Swords and lances, arrows, machine guns, and even high explosives have had far less power over the fates of nations than the typhus louse, the plague flea, and the yellow-fever mosquito. Civilizations have retreated from the plasmodium of malaria, and armies have crumbled into rabble under the onslaught of cholera spirilla, or of dysentery and typhoid bacilli."

After sketching the essay, I reread Lynd's and White's essays, in the latter unfortunately discovering that in 1937 White read an issue of the *Yale Journal of Biology & Medicine* in which the author discussed Webster's catarrh. Some springs are so dank that blossoms fall from Cornell azaleas almost as soon as they open. Still, this year the season promised warmer days, and learning that White read about Webster's ailment in the *Yale Journal* did not reduce me to wheezing. In fact I was already coughing and snorting, having suffered from sinusitis since December, something that affects me every year and is responsible, I suddenly thought, for my being an essayist rather than a novelist or lyric poet. "No man whose sinuses run gargling like spring brooks," I wrote, "could ever be a poet." On a shelf in the kitchen, I noted, stood two plastic orange containers, one filled with Clarinex tablets, the other with Levaquin capsules, each loaded with five hundred milligrams. Near them was a nasal spray, containing fluticasone furoate. In an open box that once held strawberries was a German version of a neti pot, beside it a box stuffed with five hundred packets of "Sinus Rinse" made by NeilMed. I knew that no one who wheezed as much as I did could concentrate long enough to plan a novel, and so I decided to write a piece describing the literary affects of sinusitis. I am not yet certain how to proceed and wonder if I should describe the evening I grabbed the wrong pill container and swallowed an enalapril tablet prescribed for the heart murmur of Penny, our aging Jack Russell. The next day I ran eleven miles. I felt like the last bloodroot of spring. Still no one called me "sir."

Spring Pruning

Two years ago calcium spiked in my blood, and Ken, my family doctor, sent me to a kidney specialist. I struggled through a decathlon of blood tests, at the end of which the man said, "You don't have cancer, but you probably have a benign tumor in a parathyroid. You should see an endocrinologist." Sometimes I think time a sculptor and people smooth hunks of stone, at least in their beginnings. As decades pass time batters the hunks, chiseling and riffling, hammering and prying, guttering the smoothness, carving personality and life but eventually shattering the stones so that they collapse into gravel, noticeable for a grainy moment but eventually vanishing, sinking beneath a succession of never-ending presents.

I'd endured enough files and mallets, I decided. Three years earlier a surgeon had removed some nastiness from my colon. The next fall I tore the meniscus in my right knee, and the week before Thanksgiving, a doctor scoped my knee. Immediately ahead loomed a colonoscopy and a hernia operation, this last something I delayed for nine years. Halfheartedly I attempted to see an endocrinologist in Hartford. Getting an appointment was difficult, the only opening four months away, in midsummer when Vicki and I rusticated in Nova Scotia and I wrote about fields and woods, green places that quickened the mind and honed appetite for life, for me an enchanted season not a time autumnal with white coats and scalpels.

On returning from Nova Scotia in October, I had my yearly physical. The calcium had dropped. Still I again investigated an appointment with the endocrinologist. "He doesn't have an opening until February," his secretary said. In January I went to Western Australia in hopes of writing a third book on Australia, the word *trilogy* appealing more to me than *tumor*. I returned to Connecticut on June 21. Four days later Vicki and I were in Bar Harbor waiting for the ferry to Canada. On August 25 we came back to Storrs, arriving in the evening ten hours before my first class met. Perhaps a warning should be attached to descriptions of writing courses, something like, "The surgeon general has determined that writing is dangerous to your health." Habits metastasize, even writing habits. Years of shaping pages can create the delusion that life itself can be shaped or at least its inconsecutiveness managed.

"My mind to me a kingdom is," Edward Dyer wrote at the end of the sixteenth century. The mind may be a kingdom, but it is not an empire, always capable of controlling the body. In December my throat became sore and I became hoarse, symptoms, I assumed, of a sinus infection, an ailment that bedevils me every spring. In April I saw a doctor at the University of Connecticut. In May, at the end of the semester, I planned to drive to Arkansas and spend a month at Dairy Hollow, a writers' colony in Eureka Springs. The doctor prescribed a regiment of antibiotics assuring me that they would smooth my throat for the trip. The antibiotics did not work, and on May 7, the day I gave my final examination and three days before I was off to Arkansas, I went to Mansfield Family Practice. My throat ached, and the hoarseness was worse. Ken was out of the office, and I saw Nelson Walker, an old friend from years back when our children played on the same school teams. Nelson drew blood and felt my neck.

My calcium had shot up to 12.1, normal ranging from 8.5 to 10.4, and instead of ranging between 15 and 65 my parathyroid hormone was 113, a sign of hyperparathroidism. Parathyroid glands are located in the neck, usually four of them. They make a hormone that regulates calcium in the body, keeping it from falling too low by leaching it from the bones. An overactive parathyroid makes an excessive amount of the hormone, causing blood calcium to rise and, among other matters, weakening bones. A single enlarged parathyroid was responsible for 80 percent of the cases of hyperparathyroidism, cancer causing less than one percent. That evening I drove to Willimantic and at Windham Hospital had an ultrasound on my neck. The next morning I returned to the hospital for blood tests.

After the tests I drove home along the Mansfield City Road. Near Stearns Farm a small snapping turtle hunkered down in the middle of the road, its head and legs pulled into its shell. I stopped and plucked the turtle off the asphalt. Afterward I drove to Barrow's Pond and freed the turtle in the shallows. The turtle settled wobbly for a moment, but then it shook and digging downward burrowed under a mat of water-logged oak leaves. Over the years I have rescued two score turtles from roads, and saving the snapper reassured me, an indication of good luck, I told

Vicki, adding that the turtle peed on my hands. "Defensively and out of fear," I explained, "but another sign of good luck." "In whose culture?" Vicki asked. "In mine," I answered, culture for someone my age resembling the page and being almost infinitely malleable. The next morning I turned in my grades. "High as usual?" Vicki asked. "Higher," I replied. "Astonishingly high."

A cake sweetened the grades. During the semester I taught a course in children's literature. Among the books assigned was *Alice's Adventures in Wonderland,* and to the examination Jonny and Carolyn brought a chocolate cake iced with vanilla and cut in the shape of Carroll's White Rabbit, Jonny having done the washing and scrubbing and Carolyn the cooking, "from scratch," she assured me. The rabbit's tail was a powder puff of shredded marshmallow, and the rabbit wore a pink jacket, sewn from peppermint-flavored icing and sparkly with sprinkles—just the thing to raise spirits and lure a teacher into a wonderland of generosity, something that comes less naturally as a person ages and surgeons parse away spontaneity.

The following morning, the tenth, Ken telephoned and said the ultrasound had discovered a tumor growing on a parathyroid and stretching like a glove to grasp my thyroid, a whopper-doodle four centimeters broad. Ken had contacted a surgeon and suggested an endocrinologist in Hartford, the man with whom I'd twice attempted to schedule appointments in years past and whose docket was full months in advance. Discovery of the tumor changed nothing; the first appointment I could get was on June 30. That afternoon I went to work. Three days later I had appointments in New Haven with an endocrinologist who was a professor at Yale Medical School, actually the clinical director of endocrinology, and with a surgeon at Yale specializing in endocrinology and who directed the Yale Endocrine Neoplasia Laboratory, with the former on May 27 and the latter on May 22. They were two of the best people in their specialties on the east coast. On the fourteenth I also had appointments at Yale–New Haven for another ultrasound, biopsies, and a CAT scan of my neck.

"How did you get the appointments?" Vicki asked. "Talk," I answered, "despite being hoarse." I'd spent most of the past days on the telephone, chatting with people at Yale, secretaries and office assistants who scheduled and organized, bright folks whom I made laugh and who made me laugh. Ken's office faxed the results of my tests to New Haven, and I monitored their reception, in the process becoming an individual rather than an abstract appointment. Moreover the people with whom I talked also became individuals, people with families and interests—Judy, then Josica with her bright-eyed little boy—people, oddly enough, that I began to care about and wanted to meet.

Once the fluster of arranging medical matters ended, days drifted along almost as usual. The possibility of malignancy didn't bother me. "Hell," I told friends, "I have had cancer in my behind; I might as well have it in my throat." The prospect of an operation didn't change conversation. Age had transformed the medicinal from the startling and worrying to the mundane. Moreover the funereal had become a staple of chat, so much so that I'd recently mulled having the raucous, insolent ringer on my telephone replaced by a recording of taps. When I told Vicki and the children about the operation and urged them not to worry about me, they didn't react, with the exception of Eliza who replied, "It is my right to worry about my much-loved Daddy." Later Eliza got into the carnival spirit of knife play, suggesting that I keep the tumor. "Put it in a jar and store it in the pantry beside the preserves," she said, causing me to imagine two people stumbling upon it years later. "What is this? A pickled peach?" one of the people was sure to ask, holding the jar up to a light bulb. "Damned, if I know," the other must have answered. "Maybe a truffle. Hand it to me, and I'll taste it."

I worried slightly about losing my voice. "Then what?" I said to my friend Tim. "I don't know what you'll do," Tim answered, "but your students will jump up and down gleefully, as will many people in the university, some of them your friends." I told Vicki that she would have to drive carefully when she drove me back to Storrs after the operation. I explained that only a few stitches at the base of the neck would staple my head to the rest of my body. If a tailgater bumped the back of the car, whiplash would tear my head off. "The damn thing would bounce all over the back of the car, finally rolling forward under the driver's side and getting wedged amid the levers that raise and lower the seat. The next morning you'd have to drive to East Hartford and get a mechanic at Gengras Volvo to pry my head loose, not a service covered in the warranty." "Jesus," Vicki said. For her part Vicki was a trooper, not the buff, reliable sort, but the kind associated with thunder, pails of cold rain, and leathery galoshes. Two days after returning home following the operation, I came down with the flu and spent a night upstairs vomiting. When I first became nauseated, I called Nurse Victoria, as Vicki prefers being known as whenever I sink into the feverish. Vicki was downstairs watching a television show featuring amateur dancers and did not respond. Two hours later when she came upstairs to bed, I said that I only wanted a backrub. "Backrub!" she exclaimed. "I picked you up at the hospital. Wasn't that good enough? I could have left you there." When I started to remonstrate, she interrupted, "Be quiet. I'm not taking this kind of abuse. Television has worn me out."

The prospect of an operation did not provoke anxiety, something that disappointed me slightly. Once or twice I sowed words in hopes of quickening days, for example, saying to Vicki when she was paying bills, "What does money matter to a man whose wife is a widow?" Vicki did not react. Even my dreams remained calm. One night I dreamed that I fell asleep while fishing then dreamed that I was fishing. I laughed aloud and woke up, but then, shifting my head along the shoreline of my pillow, I immediately slipped back into sleep. For a day or so I hoped worry would make me live more intensely. Spring was bright, and I imagined peering deep into the spreading green and, like a canvas bellying taut in a stream of wind, feeling the season more intensely than any time since I was a child. That did not happen. I sat in a lawn chair in the driveway and watched the fruits of red maple twitter through the sunlight, their small wings feathery and reddish gold. For a week a rug of sweet white violets covered the lawn, their perfume turning the air vanilla. I roamed the Fenton River and listened to birds. Wild pink azaleas blossomed in wetlands. Golden alexanders spread into yellow constellations, and small bouquets of blue violets bloomed beside mossy rocks. Bullfrogs thrummed, and yellow swallowtails puddled the damp along a dirt road. Male sunfish cleared the shallows of Mirror Lake into platters to entice females to lay eggs. I watched a great crested flycatcher shuttle above a beaver pond and at dusk listened to thrushes calling. Once or twice I worried that this might be my last spring. The thought, however, was as familiar as the birds and plants I saw. Each year the same thought came to mind, spurring me to break free from the armchair of easy routine and to gather rosebuds while I still had senses enough to enjoy them.

Spring bloomed lovely and long, but medical concern did not sear away the crust of past observation and invigorate sight. However, the prospect of the operation changed my behavior slightly. After classes end, I usually start a project. The project can be as long as revising a book manuscript or as short as writing book reviews. This year, though, the doctors' appointments broke May into segments. As a result I read rather than wrote. In Australia I discovered the writings of Robert Lynd, and I began picking up secondhand collections of his essays, eventually finding ten. Most of the books were first editions, not something that mattered much to me except that the editions were all of a size and on the shelf fostered the illusion that not simply reading but life itself was neat and orderly. Little things unaccountably pleased me, the pages, for example, of *Solomon in All His Glory* published in 1922 had not been cut. "Nine decades," I said to Vicki, "isn't that something?" "I don't know," she answered. "Is it?" "You bet," I answered. Although I did not realize it when I purchased the book, Lynd had autographed my copy of *The Orange Tree*, presenting it to the journalist Clement Shorter in 1926 just before Shorter's death. During May, I read Lynd's collections, marking passages with a pencil. What clung to mind were playful, not profound, bits, in *The Pleasures of Ignorance,* for example, the remark, "There is nothing that puzzles one more in a friend than if he confesses to a taste for parsnips," and in *The Orange Tree,* the observation, "One of the passages which have always made it difficult to believe in the plenary inspiration of the Scriptures is that in which we are told that God made man a little lower than the angels. It is easy enough for any of us to believe that the people whom he himself knows and loves are a little lower than the angels, but it is only through the most rose-tinted spectacles that it is possible to survey the general multitude of mankind and see in it any close resemblance to an angelic host."

The endocrinologist told me that calcium in the blood sapped energy and was associated with kidney stones, osteoporosis, and heart problems. I had not experienced any of the symptoms and felt remarkably energetic. After I told the surgeon when I met him on the twenty-second that "I'd like the operation the day before yesterday," he scheduled it for eleven o'clock in the morning on June 2. Two days later I met a friend outside the office of the English department. He looked tired, and in comparison I was bouncy. He was just back from a conference in Memphis. The conference was good, he said, adding "but that wasn't the best part of my trip." "Afterward," he recounted, "I flew to Atlanta and spent three days in the home of my college roommate. I hadn't seen him in over forty years, and I had a great time. Twice we went to French restaurants and, boy, was the food good." I then checked my mail, and my colleague walked down the hall to his office. I didn't receive any mail, and two minutes later I headed toward my office. My colleague was in his office. As I walked past, I said, "I'm glad the conference was good." "Oh," he said, "but that wasn't the best part of my trip. Afterward I flew to Atlanta and spent three days in the home of my college roommate. I hadn't seen him in over forty years, and I had a great time. Twice we went to French restaurants and, boy, was the food good." "My god! Has the poor man lost his marbles?" Vicki exclaimed when I described the encounter to her. "No, of course not," I said, feeling perky, "he's just a good teacher, and all good teachers are repetitious."

I felt so good that I entered the Iron Horse Half-Marathon, run on a Sunday in Simsbury two days before my operation. I did not tell Vicki, and the morning of the race crept out of the house at five o'clock. My right hip and lower back ached, but small pains had never slowed me, and when I saw a bed of iris near the starting line, I felt confident, iris being one of my favorite flowers. Alas flowers bloom and blow, and for the first time in a race, I broke down. After eleven miles my lower back shattered in a splint of pain, doubling me over and forcing me to stop running and walk. Despite being bent like a staple, I tried to jog across the finish line. I failed. I couldn't stand straight, and as I approached the line, I leaned over more and more from the waist, so much so that my nose sank close to my knees no matter how I tried to raise my head. Three yards before the finish, I collapsed headfirst, whacking the asphalt. Blood spurted from my right eyebrow; the crowd gasped, and two police-men and four members of a rescue squad sprinted to my aid. I waved them off, struggled to a crouch, and waddled across the line. A wooden fence ran beside the finish. I staggered over to rest on it. Unfortunately I was so twisted that, when I leaned onto the top rail, my head flopped over the far side. I could not lever myself back up and stand. As a result my head became a heavy anchor and pulled me over the fence, and I fell again, this time landing on the top of my head, my legs waggling above me in the air. Again the rescue squad raced to my aid and embarrass-ment. After I assured them that my heart was fine and that my wife was in the crowd and would drive me home, they left me alone, all except one policeman. For ten minutes he followed me as I limped toward my car. "I'm not stalking you," he said. "I just want to be sure you are all right."

I did not receive any sympathy when I got back to Storrs. Words like *jackass* and *nincompoop* seasoned Vicki's greeting, sprinkled around the ends of sentences exclamations such as "two days before your opera-tion" and "have you a brain?" Actions are mysterious and mycorrhizal, their roots thrusting through the underground of personality and draw-ing sustenance from and supplying it to sundry hosts. I cannot explain why I ran a half-marathon two days before the operation. Neither do I really know why I waited over two years to have my parathyroid exam-ined. Every Memorial Day I attend the parade in Mansfield Center and afterward walk with townsfolk to the hilltop graveyard. I never listen to the speeches, however, but instead wander the silent downhill fringes of the graveyard, looking at wildflowers in the grass at the edge of the woods—geranium, chickweed, yellow winter cress, the first purple clover, and sometimes in the green damp blue flag. Even the gentlest words cannot muffle the drums under the speeches, at least to my ears. I wish I did not feel compelled to separate from my neighbors. Do I roam apart because my family were Quakers for almost two hundred years, their attitudes toward life and peace, coursing through heredity, not shaping all subsequent generations but surfacing in me to influence my attitudes? I will never know.

What I do know, however, is that I made five trips to New Haven, three before the operation, one for the operation, and one after, Vicki accompanying me twice, on the initial trip then on again my being admitted to Yale–New Haven Hospital. The drive was sixty-three miles long, and the numbers of the roads cling to mind like Band-Aids, 275, 32, 44 then a series of I's, 384, 84, and 91, this last reached by crossing the Charter Oak Bridge, CT-15. I drove early in the morning to avoid traffic around Hartford and New Haven. I wasn't always successful. Skeins of trucks shuttled across highways, cars weaving between them, sometimes waving in loose threads, other times breaking and piling close to one another in knots of hoods and trunks, taillights flaring. Like a Luddite, I resisted the traffic's mechanical insistence that I speed. North of New Haven at Mt. Carmel on 91, I got into and stayed in the slow righthand lane until I turned into the city at Exit 1, the two lanes to my left buckled with vehicles jerking toward I-95 South. The drive from Storrs usually took slightly under an hour and a half, the quickest lasting seventy-four minutes, this for an 8:00 appointment with the surgeon six days after the operation. On that morning I left home at 5:00. At 6:14 I parked my car in New Haven.

I'm never on time. I am always early. I had two appointments on the fourteenth, the first day I drove to New Haven, the initial appointment at 12:45 for biopsies and an ultrasound in the Doctors Building on Church Street then at 2:00 a CAT scan at the East Pavilion of Yale–New Haven Hospital, a fifteen-minute walk away. Because there wasn't much time between appointments, I worried that I'd be late for or even miss the scan. Consequently I decided to leave Storrs shortly after breakfast, thinking that if I showed up ahead of schedule a secretary might squeeze the tests in early. Vicki and I squabbled over the departure, but I prevailed with her and in the doctor's office. In fact on my arrival after I talked to the secretaries, I jumped to the top of both appointment books. By 2:00 the tests at both the Doctors Building and the hospital were over, and Vicki and I met Edward for lunch at a Thai restaurant. On the twenty-seventh I showed up for a 10:30 appointment at 8:15. By 9:00 I had seen the doctor. The biopsies nipped, then scratched, and were almost unnoticeable, although by the end of the third one I was glad they were over. During the CAT scan a liquid was inserted in the vein of my right arm, warming my head for a moment and making me sleepy. I tried to keep track of tests run on me, two ultrasounds, for example. For a while, beginning in Storrs, I counted the tubes of blood pulled from my arms, these to measure, among others, basic metabolism, calcium, plasma parathyroid hormone, and vitamin D metabolism. The drawings were painless, but I lost track around sixteen, the number beginning to make me queasy, as did a couple of nurses who had to shovel for veins after drilling dry wells in my arms. Moreover I couldn't decide how to count an IV, say, one that had a stop cock on it, through which water or anesthetic could be dripped. No matter the total of drawings, for a month the remnants of adhesive clung to the insides of my arms, brown and rolling up like miniature rugs.

After eating lunch, Edward, Vicki, and I went to Atticus on Chapel Street and drank a cappuccino. Because my other appointments were also early in the day, I met Edward twice more at Atticus. One morning I dropped by the Yale English department to talk to a man with whom I taught at Dartmouth and whom I had not seen since 1978. Twice I went to the Yale Center for British Art to view "Paintings from the Reign of Victoria," an exhibition assembled from the Royal Holloway Collection in London. On display were several famous paintings, notably William Powell Frith's panorama of a crowd in Paddington Station, *The Railway Station*, 1862. Whenever I visit an exhibition, I imagine taking a picture home and hanging it in the living room. My house is small. Ceilings are low, and chests line rooms, above them knick-knacks from my travels, leaving no space for the sublime or the massive. And so I always cart away a comparatively small painting, usually a landscape or a conversation piece, a canvas that might start a sentence but that would never overwhelm, smothering table talk. From the Yale Center, I decided to lift Briton Rivière's *Sympathy*, 1877, depicting a small girl dressed in black patent-leather shoes with bows on the toes and wearing black stockings and a ruffled blue dress. The girl sat on the top step of a stairwell. A worn Oriental runner covered the stairs, and the railing to the girl's right was heavy and dark. The girl's right hand supported her chin, and her eyes gazed upward, her mind occupied by a scolding. Leaning against her on her left was her companion, a white dog, ears flattened, not cowed, but collapsed in sympathy with the girl's mood.

The operation was scheduled for 11:00 in the morning and labeled "minimally invasive parathyroid surgery." The surgeon said the operation would probably last only half an hour and he would use a local anesthetic. Average blood loss was less than an ounce, and because the risk of infection was low, antibiotics were not necessary. A small chance existed that nerves in the neck that control the vocal cords could be affected, a concern because I was hoarse and in April a friend had lost his voice after undergoing a thyroid operation. The hospital was supposed to telephone on the first, confirming the time of the operation. No one contacted me, so that evening I called the hospital, learning that the operation had been shifted to one o'clock in the afternoon, the surgeon's last operation of the day. "Oh, dear," I told Vicki, "the size of the tumor means the operation will last longer than half an hour." "How do you know?" she said, "I don't see M.D. after your name." "The letters are there," I said. "Put on your reading glasses."

Several people waited in the lounge outside the ambulatory surgery center. Couples sat quietly. A heavy man wearing blue jeans and earphones sang aloud. I heard snatches of verses, first the "banana-fana" song then "Sugar Pie, Honey Bunch." A Hispanic family gathered around a woman who said, "I've got the best surgeon, but God is in control." In the center itself a nurse inserted an IV in my arm, and I put on a johnny. Vicki tied the laces in the back for me, and I kept on my underwear, its pattern blue and white checks. "Nice underpants," a cheery woman said later. At 12:58 I walked into the operating room. Six people welcomed me, all dressed in turquoise and good natured. I stretched out on a table, my head lower than the rest of my body and resting in a doughnut. Oddly I looked forward to tracking the operation. I recall looking up, my eyes shielded by a flimsy blue cloth a foot or so above my head. I felt the first cut on my neck. "Wow," I thought. But that is all I remember. The quick minimally invasive operation stretched to an hour and a half. A breathing tube was run down my throat; the local anesthetic became general, and along with the enlarged parathyroid, the surgeon removed the right lobe of my thyroid. For the record the tumor wasn't malignant. But it was "astonishingly large" and weighed 1,500 milligrams. I woke up in the recovery room. 'You looked sweet," Vicki said, "your eyes were big and moist."

Instead of going home after the operation, I stayed the night, in room 412 on the sixth floor, my roommate having been there a week after having stomach surgery, a track of stitches running from his naval to his sternum. In my arm was an IV, water dripping through it, making movement awkward until 12:17 that night when a nurse disconnected the IV. The tube remained in my arm, however, until I left, filling with blood and curving pasted under my elbow like a thin parasitical worm. From collarbone to Adam's apple my neck was purple and swollen, the swelling rumpling in layers and looking like a stack of small inner tubes. My chest was darker; the skin above my sternum more black than purple, a bruise running ten or eleven inches from right to left. Breathing hurt, though I said it didn't, and my throat was sore, making eating so unpleasant that for dinner I only ordered a ginger ale and a small tub of raspberry Jell-O.

Shortly after Vicki returned to Storrs, Edward came by, bringing a book for me to read, *Quartered Safe Out Here,* George MacDonald Fraser's account of fighting in Burma in 1944 and '45 as the war ended and the Japanese forces crumbled. I stayed up and read the book, finishing it early in the morning. Sleeping was impossible. People checked on me throughout the night, taking my pulse and temperature and always asking my name and birthday and sometimes my address. During visits to the doctors' offices and my stay in the hospital, I signed books of forms, the same forms repeatedly, many informing me of my rights, none of which I care about. At times I'm a loner, but I am not private. What people think or say about me, so long as they do the latter behind my back, doesn't matter. In truth I pay little attention to either compliments or insults. Actually compliments make me more uncomfortable than insults, the latter more often than not making me laugh rather than wince.

Once the drip was disconnected, I roamed the floor. Posted on broadsides on the walls of rooms was a list of the hospital's goals, one of which was "I will create a great first impression." The nurses and their aids did create good impressions. For my part I was a nuisance, a wanderer who refused to stay in bed but who instead circled the nurses' stations, sometimes creeping, other times almost skipping, varying the pace for my own enjoyment. I was also a medical hazard. A number of people working on the floor had originally come from the South and either had family living in the South or planned to move there when they retired. On being asked where I was from, I started telling stories. Soon a group gathered about me chuckling, more people than ever read my books. "Suppose a patient had a heart attack while you were carrying on and nobody noticed," Vicki said later. "Wouldn't you have felt terrible?" "No," I said, quoting Robert Lynd's *The Green Man* (1928), "The only fatal error in a writer is to be uninteresting."

In truth I was disappointed as the operation and the stay in the hospital were not as stimulating as I thought they would be. Indeed throughout May I remained mellow, unconcerned once the calendar of appointments was set. None of my feelings ran, as Wordsworth put it, too deep for tears or better perhaps coursed deep enough to tap into capillary thought. The worst, and most interesting and immediate, effect of the operation was that the anesthetic made it difficult to urinate. A nurse took an ultrasound of my bladder and told me that I might have to stay another day in the hospital if I couldn't relieve myself. Urinating was painful and slow. To help things along I stood outside my door and jumped up and down. Supposedly I couldn't leave until my bladder contained less than 200 cubic centimeters of urine. Jumping, and shaking that I am not going to describe, reduced the number to 244. At that point I thought I was on the way home, but then the figure rose to 351. Three ultrasounds are enough for any bladder, and so I increased the energy of my jumps, accompanying them with a chorus of whoopees.

Visible madness is unnerving and irritating. Vicki arrived, and within an hour, she was driving me back to Storrs. With me I carried a prescription for extrastrength Tums in case the calcium level in my blood dropped precipitously, a sign of that being numbness around the mouth and tingling fingers, neither of which happened. I also had a prescription for Tylenol loaded with codeine, a pain killer. Vicki had this prescription filled, but I refused to take the pills, saying I did not want to become a dope fiend. On the way home, Vicki stopped at the university dairy bar, and I ate a cup of chocolate brownie fudge ice cream. Usually I have the child's cup, but I decided I deserved a treat so I indulged myself and ordered the regular adult cup. For her part Vicki had a cone, one scoop coconut, the other caramel, "a horror," I said.

"Now that the operation is over," Vicki said as we sat in the dairy bar, "what are you going to do with yourself?" For ten or so days after the operation I felt tired. Moreover my hip hurt from the half-marathon, and I didn't run. I went for long walks, one morning through clouds of mountain laurel atop a ridge near Bolton Notch, another day noticing flowers, foxglove beardtongue for the first time. Two old friends had strokes, almost simultaneously. They'd taught at the same college for decades. While one of the men lost his voice, the other became convinced that his colleague had long served the CIA as an assassin, teaching being only a ruse and attending literary conventions the cover for assignments. On hearing about the two men, I shook my head. I decided I needed a cause or a project to awaken my remaining parathyroids, something comparable to Robert Lynd's criticism of milk drinking in *Solomon in All His Glory.* "For some extraordinary reason, the Government while shutting the public-houses during several hours of the day, permits the sale of milk at all hours," Lynd wrote. "The early morning glass of milk has in consequence become a habit with thousands of people and especially, it is to be feared, with young people. There is no legal age-limit for buying milk as there is for buying alcohol or tobacco. One result of this is that enough money is spent on milk every year to pay for the up-keep of the Army and Navy." As an eminently reasonable man, like me of course, Lynd stressed that he did not want to discuss the "ravages of the milk habit" in detail, observing that good men and women took different views of the subject and warning that "it may be infinitely more harmful to suppress a habit than to tolerate it, even if it does a considerable amount of harm." Hence, he concluded, he would be reluctant "to see any but moral pressure brought to bear on milk-drinkers. They should be dealt with by the clergy rather than by the police." "Maybe," I told Vicki after reading her the excerpt from Lynd, "I can streamline the production of boiled eggs by teaching chickens to swim in hot water." "You are back to your old self," Vicki said, sighing. "Not quite but almost," I said. "By the way," I continued, "did you read in today's paper about the monstrously big pipsqueak who was just a yard shy of eight feet tall?"

Puffing

Last March the Oxford University Press asked me to write a puff for the book jacket of Stanley Fish's *Save the World on Your Own Time*. I have written a library of blurbs, so many that my friend Josh has nicknamed me "Puff Adder." Moments determine words. When I received the request from Oxford, I was living alone in a small flat in Perth. Some days I did not speak. I spent mornings in the Reid Library at the University of Western Australia. Every afternoon, I jogged for two hours. For dinner I drank orange juice or tea and ate bread and cheese, sometimes varying meals by dumping a small can of beans or tuna over rice. After dinner I read. Rarely are simple things simple. I had pared my life down in hopes of writing a luxuriant book. Additionally I had not taught in eleven months. Amid the wintry fabric of scribbling, the pleasures of teaching had slipped from my mind. I worried that I wouldn't finish my manuscript before returning to the classroom. In dark moments I pondered retirement and fretted about school things, dreading having to grade papers and dealing with students intent on achieving high, unearned grades, albeit these last characters were more fictional than real. Rarely have students nagged me about grades because, as I tell friends, I give all students half a grade higher than they could ever imagine receiving.

In his book Fish wrote that college and university teachers could "legitimately" do two things: first, "introduce students to bodies of knowledge and traditions of inquiry that had not previously been part of their experience," and second, "equip those same students with the analytical skills—of argument, statistical modeling, laboratory procedure— that will enable them to move confidently within those traditions and to engage in independent research after a course is over." To shine a taper on a single quotation, on one strand of the rich fabric of Fish's book, distorts and does as great a disservice to *Save the World on Your Own Time* as a classroom does to the complexity of life. Nevertheless the book appealed to the me in Perth who wanted to jettison the smog of amor-phous matters that sap energy and undermine writing, concerns about politics, morality, and social change among others, the sorts of things that turn university days smoky. The sharp edge of Fish's thought appeared admirable. In comparison my classroom stumblings seemed lazy and self-indulgent, emotional and unconsidered. After reading the book I felt guilty, almost ashamed, and so in the blurb I wrote, "Exhilarating, the thought polished and white-hot, this book makes the reader think and often wince, especially teachers like me who have aged out of the intel-lectual into the easy and congenial. A close reading of *Save the World* should purge much nonsense from classrooms."

I have now returned to Connecticut. The moment has changed. I still run, only every other day, however. Alas Vicki's meals sprawl beyond delight into excess, and I am putting on weight. When I read at night, a dog sleeps in my lap, usually Jack but sometimes Penny or Suzy. Last weekend Vicki and I drove across the northeast part of the state, visiting artists' studios. We bought three paintings, all landscapes riotous with color. The fall semester has ended, and on Wednesday I turned in my grades, only one C in the lot. I still admire Fish's book, but I no longer feel guilty about my teaching. Instead of wincing at my performances in the classroom, I now wince at my self-deprecatory blurb.

The ways of learning are many and various, and I am not constitu-tionally capable of high seriousness. "The only truth I can state," John Mason Brown wrote in *Still Seeing Things,* "is a personal one. Accord-ingly, I have no other choice than to write personally. What a man is is the basis of what he dreams and thinks, accepts and rejects, feels and perceives. It is, too, the stuff from which he writes." For my part I have no choice but to teach personally, my perceptions and dreams shaping not only my analysis of the books I assign but also my perceptions of the kids, the boys and girls, who enroll in my classes. For most students that seems good enough. "I don't know what I have learned, or if I have learned anything at all," a student recently wrote me. "You were the in-spiration for many of my writings this semester, the provoker of many thoughts. . . . All semester, I wanted to devour your mind, searching for something that I probably could not recognize nor understand anyway."

Praise makes me uncomfortable. It makes me a doubter, and I won-der if I am just an actor strutting the stage, my personality and manner-isms distracting students from real thought. However, I teach English, and in part a student's not being sure if he has learned anything from me is appealing. If I taught anatomy, matters would be different. Confusion of the colon with the mitral and aortic valves would lead to interesting bypasses though I doubt they would relieve coronary congestion.

I profess to solve no problems, thinking that most solutions are obtained only after peeling complexity away, leaving behind distortion. Indeed I think solutions preludes to new problems. I am a southerner, and because I loved the South in which I grew up, only to realize in my early twenties that the society that nurtured me was raised upon the unspeakable injustice of segregation, I am a doubter and a questioner. I have no goals. I strive only to be interesting. In weak moments I imagine that my remarks might startle students into thought or appreciation. I have no methodology. I don't teach according to system. Instead I cope with what the classroom tosses at me, this more often than not influenced by doings outside class, a broken hot-water heater, a friend's sickness, a child's worries, or, for example, what I am writing, hammering into illusion for the page. I studiously reject the programmatic, especially schools of literary criticism, which are dandy for jump-starting academic careers but which plane the infinite variety out of living and literature.

I wish I could endow my students with good luck. But that is not possible. Some days I know that discipline and hard work determine good luck. Other days I know that idleness determines good luck. Some mornings I believe that skills are necessary to success. Perhaps, though, a person with few skills fares better than a person with many, his life not narrowed by achievement. For my part I could do nothing well as a child, aside, maybe, from getting along with people. I could not climb trees or do a somersault. Swimming came only after I was fished out of a couple of pools. I was a terrible athlete. Moreover I am tone deaf and color blind. My palate is as sensitive as sixty-grit sandpaper. Because I could do little well, I was free to be interested in many things. Skill did not impose focus upon me, and I roamed waywardly. I remain wayward. In class I am unable to temper the display not only of personality but also of the lives I have led and the life I am presently leading, something Fish argues should be done on my, not a school's, time. He is, of course, right for himself and for many teachers, but not for me, and not for my students, at least not right for all my students all the time.

A teacher can never know his influence or the lack thereof. Even when a student declares that a teacher has influenced him, it probably isn't so. More than likely the student has succumbed to platitudinous thinking. Instead of actually mulling the formative, he has slipped into the socially acceptable and socially trite, finding nonexistent cause and effect in the fool's gold of popular imagination. Moreover, if I really thought I influenced lives, I would be too frightened to crawl out of bed in the morning. Perhaps teaching is easier if one binds personality and remains within the strict academic bounds that Fish delineates. Still I doubt it. What I do know is that, when one leaps those bounds, teaching becomes worrying and exhausting, perhaps riskier, this last, I suspect, more to others than to one's self. This past semester one of my students decided to stop playing intercollegiate athletics. Although she held a scholarship for two and a half years, she had not gotten into a game, something of which I was ignorant. In an essay she wrote, "You inadvertently empowered me to make my decision. During class you said something to the effect that 'the good thing about failure is that it sets you free.' While I don't think myself a failure or the time I spent as an athlete wasted, the phrase struck a chord. If I decided to quit, I was free. I was free from bouts of depression and free from the dark feelings of failure that followed me everywhere." In truth many things convinced the girl to stop playing, among them perhaps literature itself. In the course students read Thoreau's *Walden,* and the girl ended her autobiographical account writing, "I was free to live other lives," an echo of Thoreau's statement, "I left the woods for as good a reason as I went there. Perhaps it seemed to me that I had several more lives to live."

Seining out threads of influence is difficult, the results usually woven into fiction rather than into truth. Occasionally, however, matters are almost clear. "I used to walk around campus and ignore the spare change on the ground," a student wrote in a class I taught on the personal essay. "I even threw the pennies I received as change away onto the street. As I threw them, I said to people that questioned me, 'Pennies are someone else's dream.' It was pretty idealistic of me to think that the pennies I threw away were being found by people with serious needs. Through the course of this class I found that my abandoned pennies were being scooped up by Sam Pickering."

I pluck pennies from the ground, and earlier in the term I had talked about my little coin hunts, noting that the campus was rich with copper game as students rarely harvested pennies. During one safari, I recounted, I found twenty-seven pennies. I also said that on the infrequent occasions when I accompanied Vicki to the grocery, I did not go inside the store but instead remained outside roaming the parking lot, searching for pennies. "Something that embarrasses Vicki," I said, "but that seems to me remarkably sensible." After the final class the girl came to my office. In her hand was a small leather bag, a drawstring tight across the mouth. Inside were 141 pennies. "All the pennies I found on the ground this semester—they are for you," the girl explained, handing me the bag, adding before she left my office, "the best hunting is outside the bookstore. Pennies like to camouflage themselves in the leaves around bicycle stands." Faculty are not supposed to accept presents from students, but the girl insisted I take the pennies, so I took them, deciding to donate them to the English department's "general fund." After the girl left, I started down the hall toward the English office. I stopped halfway. "To hell with it," I muttered. "You are sixty-seven. Why not live recklessly for once," I said aloud then continued walking, passing the office. I strode out of the building and crossed the campus to the university museum. In the Arts Café I bought a medium-sized cup of coffee, the pennies covering slightly more than 85 percent of the price.

Despite not knowing how my classes affect students, I am aware of how students affect me. For the record I am not one of those sappy nincompoops whom I see quoted in magazines devoted to pedagogy saying, "I only hope students will learn as much from me this semester as I learn from them." Students have never taught me anything, and if they had something to teach, I would not want to learn it. I am, though, an autumnal man burdened with chores thick, I sometimes think, to quote John Milton, Fish's great literary love, as "Leaves that strow the Brooks in Vallombrosa." Well, that's an exaggeration. Still little things that once seemed of a minute now often seem of an hour. Once upon a time I could write five letters of recommendation and a book review then begin an essay in a sitting. Now after two recommendations I need to slug myself back into sentences with a pot of English breakfast tea.

Instead of teaching me, students startle me, not into knowledge but into awareness, polishing touchstones of recognition that have long lain tarnished in memory. In a story a student described a girl watching a man neatening his wife's grave. The girl's mother was dead, but because she disliked accompanying her father to the graveyard, she visited her mother's grave alone. During these visits she described her life, "revealing things that would have disappointed her mother." She spoke out loud, "wondering if her mother could hear her, or a god, or the family on the other side of the cemetery." Because death freed the living, she spoke confidently. "She could say anything without fearing a reaction from her mother. The girl had learned during infancy to distrust the living, and therefore she did not love them. Because she did not love them, she did not cry for them. Two years after her mother's death, the girl realized her mother was dead. She realized she could love her and cry for her. Her healthiest relationship was with her deceased mother." The story struck me as wise beyond the page. I talk to my parents every day, not something I did when they were alive. Like the girl, I speak aloud. I describe my worries and tell them about their grandchildren. I tell them that I miss them. I tell them that if I knew I could meet them in another life, I would embrace death open armed and smiling with joy.

Only nitwits suckled on pasty psychobabble believe education therapeutic. Nevertheless students cheer me, and a couple of hours in a classroom invigorates, making me, in Thoreau's words, "throw off sleep" and if not trip "the light fantastick toe," at least perking me up enough to wander field and page, in the latter catching words on the wing, in the former studying the wrinkled beauty of flowers. "Five years ago," a student wrote describing Thanksgiving, "my uncle stood to make a toast. We thought he was going to say how proud he was of his children and sing their praises. But we were surprised. At the time none of my cousins had boyfriends or girlfriends, a rare state of being. My uncle said that he was thankful all his children had broken up with their 'insignificant significant others.' Now every year my uncle makes the same toast no matter if my cousins are dating someone, and the dinner always ends with one of my cousins crying or storming off from the table."

"A teacher wrote in my high school yearbook that I had the potential to change the world," another student wrote. "At graduation, our valedictorian quoted Mahatma Gandhi, telling members of the class to 'be the change you want to see in the world.' These comments astounded me because I have trouble changing my Brita filter every three months. I will stare at the blinking light on my dashboard for weeks until someone else gets my car's oil changed. I sometimes forget to change my socks. I don't understand why people, especially Americans, emphasize change so much. I like to keep things they way they are. I follow the 'if it ain't broke, don't fix it' philosophy, whereas my teachers and classmates maintain the 'if it ain't broke, break it' mentality. I am most comfortable when I know exactly what is going to happen. I don't mind going to church because I can recite the mass in both English and Latin without having to think about the words. I never expect the priest to abandon his ceremonious, 'Take and Eat' speech in favor of the informal, 'Snack time.'"

Praise is a sweet that doesn't provide sustenance. Nevertheless sometimes a student writes something for which I wish he would give me credit, this despite my realizing that celebratory words are sugar, refined by distortion. One of my students spent the summer of her twelfth year studying box turtles and damselflies and, during the warm months, brightly growing. "Everything was new and unknown that summer," she recalled.

"There was excitement in everything fresh, like being caught in a dark moment with an adolescent boy, who for the first time made me feel like I had lost control of my limbs. I could hear a whip-poor-will calling in the distance, and my heart felt heavy in my chest." When I was twelve, I spent the summer on my grandfather's farm in Virginia. One day an older girl stood at the door of a red barn. She undid the top buttons on her blouse and beckoned to me to follow her inside. I didn't hear a whip-poor-will. I was too scared to hear anything. My heart wasn't heavy. Instead my feet were light, and I ran home.

Obviously much teaching occurs outside classrooms, in talks or in books such as *Save the World on Your Own Time* among others. During a semester I receive wads of letters and e-mails asking for advice of a kind I never proffer in a course. In class, thoughts about living arise from the readings I assign, Richard Jefferies declaring, for example, "Pondering deeply and for long upon the plants, the living things (myself, too, as a physical being): upon the elements, on the holy miracle, water; the holy miracle, sunlight; the earth, and the air, I come at last—and not without, for a while, sorrow—to the inevitable conclusion that there is no object, no end, no purpose, no design, and no plan; no anything, that is."

Teachers lead different lives simultaneously. In class I respond quickly to questions. At home my response to letters is slower and more considered. The considered, however, is not truer than the spontaneous. While spontaneity errs on the side of abandon, the mulled errs on the side of caution. "You are a personal hero of mine," a teenager wrote. "Not hero, so much as an inspiration. You broke the mold to a different method of teaching, writing, creativity, imagination." "Your teaching reminded me so much of the English teacher I had my freshman year of high school. He opened our minds to so many things and made us think. He told us we have no limitations; there are no limitations for us. We can do anything if we are determined enough, if we are passionate enough." My correspondent ended by asking for "tips on how to motivate one's self on writing a novel." *Inspiration* is a word I do not say; in fact at the beginning of each semester I banish it from the classroom. Moreover I have never bamboozled kids into believing lies. All people have limitations. Still, as Richard Rodriguez notes, the young man's optimism is just as true as the old man's pessimism. And so in answering my correspondent, I praised her bouncing prose after which I tempered her enthusiasm by describing how I wrote, outlining and revising endlessly. "On my desk," I wrote, "are 470 handwritten pages, front and back, an account of 6 months I spent in Australia earlier this year. For seven weeks I have spent most of the time I am not in class typing and revising my way through the pages, 21.2% so far. The going is slow and tedious." I advised her not to attempt a novel but instead to wander the out of doors with a notebook and pencil. "Motivation," I continued, "usually stems from observation. After your walk, write a page describing what you saw."

The girl did not answer me. I didn't expect her to. I was not sufficiently enthusiastic. No matter, I was answering a letter written by a man who had taken a course with me five years ago. "I am writing at this time out of sheer desperation for career advice," he explained, adding, "Prof. Pickering, do you have a moment to offer any advice as to how I can get from nowhere to the type of career you have had?" I wrote a long answer even though explaining the course of a life is impossible. Indeed what a stranger thinks success may in truth be failure. Advising anyone was difficult, I said, because "advice is only advice." The man dreamed of writing, so I told him to write. To that end I urged him to join a writing group. "Would that I had a key that spun tumblers magically and unlocked doors to happiness," I wrote, adding, "But I don't." Like the girl, the man did not answer me, but again I was too busy to care, replying to another correspondent who asked me whether he should return to college at age thirty-one.

Amid many differences I suppose Mr. Fish and I share a thought or two, so I won't recant my blurb. *Save the World* is good, and so is my blurb, just right for the book even if the teacher I describe as me is not someone who makes me wince but who is a good fellow, content in the classroom and in life, someone with whom I would not mind sharing a pitcher of "spicy nut-brown ale." Still I am not sure the author of *Save the World* would enjoy "To Catch a Fish," a piece written by one of my students. Of course the piece delighted me. "Creating an aquarium is like creating a living ecosystem," a boy wrote. "It may not be creating life, but it is creating something in which life can exist. God is the same way. He may not have created humans from nothing, but he created the proper environment for life to flourish. When I look at the fishes in my tank, I wonder if they consider me a god. When my fishes see me, they rub their noses into the glass as if they were trying to swim to me. Experts say that fishes do this because they are conditioned to do so to get food. But this might be their way of worshipping me. When people are hungry, they pray for food. Fishes behave the same way. They are begging the 'Greater Being' to provide for them. Unlike fishes humans cannot see their provider. My mother always tells me that God is watching me. I do not know if this is true or not. All I know is that I like to check on my fishes once in a while and watch them to see how they behave. God probably does the same thing as well."

"A humdinger, a jim-dandy," I said at dinner after reading the paragraph to Vicki. "What?" Vicki said, reacting as I imagine Mr. Fish would react. "What in the pluperfect hell?" Of course the odds are pretty good that a long-term wife won't like the things her husband enjoys. And, reader, you might guess this: I had aquariums when I was young. I stocked them with schools of fish: black mollies and red swordtails; neon tetras; white kissing gouramis; loaches stripped orange and black like Princeton scarves; hatchets, their appearance responsible for their name; zebra- and angelfish; and then guppies, dear, dear guppies, the long tails of the males dappled with color. My hatcheries did not last long. One winter when I was ten or eleven, an ice storm knocked down the power lines in my neighborhood, and Mother and Father and I were forced to move out of our house for a week. When we returned, all my fish were dead, the aquariums little ponds silver with ice.

Post Operative

In September, as the old story puts it, two bulls met outside a barn. "How was your summer?" the first bull asked. "Splendid," the second bull lowed, rubbing his hide against a door jam. "I spent the vacation in the lowlands up to my hocks in clover, drinking spring water that tasted like oats. The flies weren't bad, and on muggy days I dozed in the shade under a pair of sugar maples. Even better I wasn't alone. A herd of young heifers frisked about, always eager to kick up their hooves without giving half a moo for tomorrow's silage." "But enough about Arcadia," the bull said, fond ruminations making him roll his cud over slowly, "how was your vacation?" "Oh, Lord," the other bull replied. "I spent the months behind barbed wire on a rocky hillside, drinking water ranker than a salt lick. Horse flies bit like bullets, and the only tree on the hill was a spindly, half-dead redbud. Even worse, I didn't have a single cow for company, just one damned old steer that kept talking about his operation."

The end of June had arrived. Instead of snuffing the sweet air of Nova Scotia, I was in Connecticut, enduring a sour barrage of postoperative tests. Moreover my conversation had devolved into talk sharp with cuttings and slicings. For the young chatter about scalpels and syringes is dull. People of a certain age, however, no longer converse earnestly about breast feeding or maunder about education, debating the merits of sundry schools. We have jettisoned dreams of clambering to the tops of mountains, pulling ourselves over scree so sharp that it rends habit and ruptures convention. Instead we take cruises. At night we drink a single glass of wine and talk about health and death, "our topics," my friend Josh said to me recently, "not athletics or interior decorating, but kidneys and colons, livers and thyroids."

We had aged, Josh lectured, into the pleasures of superficiality. Psychology now seemed ridiculous. No longer did we attempt to solve problems, finally realizing that solutions were usually worse than problems themselves. On something's going wrong, the mature merely nodded, the head bobbing evanescent, lasting only until the telephone's next tinkle, the sound a harbinger of grim but often paradoxically entertaining news. To illustrate his point, Josh cited an account he'd read in the *Carthage Courier*. The article described the reaction of a mother in Maggart on learning that her youngest child had slipped through the seat in the outhouse and, splashing into the margarine below, had sunk out of sight, only a smattering of bubbles marking the spot where he disappeared. On reaching the privy, the mother thrust her head through the seat and studied the matter below. "We might be able dig him out, but I ain't sure it's worth it," she said, pulling her head up and addressing her husband. "Oh, hell," she continued, wiping her left arm across her forehead and pointing to the hole, "just leave him there. It's easier to get another baby than to clean that one up, even if we could fetch him."

Josh's visit cheered me. I had forgotten Vicki's and my thirtieth wedding anniversary. I was bothered, not because the oversight bruised Vicki, but because forgetfulness was an early sign of dementia. In truth I didn't worry much because I had not remembered any of our previous twenty-nine anniversaries. Actually the more I considered the matter, the better I felt. Recalling the anniversary would have been out of character and thus a bad sign, a symptom of radical, probably deadly, mental deterioration. To atone for my habitual oversight, however, the following Sunday I treated Vicki to breakfast at Jodi's Place in Willimantic. We both had two eggs sunny-side up, patty sausage, whole-wheat toast, coffee, and hash browns, onions twisting like vines through this last. The onions raised my anniversary spirits, and I decided to make a day of it, after breakfast driving to the flea market at the Mansfield Drive-In where Vicki bought herself a present, paying seven dollars for an iron skillet. Early in the afternoon we ambled over to the Benton Art Museum on campus and watched a movie starring Harold Lloyd. We were the only people at the movie. We sat on a couch on the first floor landing, and Vicki said the movie was "cozy, just right for an anniversary." Later we walked the dogs in the woods below the cow barn. On the way home I bought Indian takeout, a vegetable biryani, which we ate while watching one of Agatha Christie's Inspector Poirot mysteries on public television. "A pearl of a day," Josh remarked after I described our doings to him.

Josh subscribes to a score of newspapers, and his visits are informative as well as therapeutic. He does not take the *Wall Street Journal* or the *New York Times* because, as he explains, he wants to read about "real Americans." Much of what Josh tells me is lifted from papers published in the South and, to anyone not born in the area, must seem apocryphal. Recently the Georgia legislature debated expenditures for higher education, a full report appearing in the *Atlanta Constitution*. "I don't want to give money to no college," the representative from Elberton declared, "because I've heard tell that men and women *matriculate* in broad daylight, the Lord help us, right there before everybody." "That ain't the worst of it," a member from Waycross added. "Them boys and girls use the same *curriculum,* and they don't care who knows it neither." "Hellfire," the representative from Griffin interrupted, "That ain't anywheres near the worst. Everyone of them girl students is required to show her *thesis* to the professor." The outlook for the bill was dark until a representative from Moultrie shifted the subject of the debate, attacking teachers, saying professors got paid a lot of money for not much work. "Professors," an enlightened Democrat from Lumber City replied, ending the discussion, "is a lot like bulls. They may not be on the job for many hours at a time, but what they does is mighty important."

The next morning I received an article clipped from the *Clarion Ledger* in Mississippi sent by my college chum Jimmy Brown. "I want you and your sophisticated friends in Connecticut to be aware of how we in Mississippi elevate nature to the highest levels," Jimmy wrote. Three times a year, the article recounted, a group of friends went snake catching, pulling water snakes from the shallows of ponds and along the banks of small rivers. The snakes provided an occasion to spend a night in the woods, camping and cooking, and probably telling tales similar to those Josh tells me. "A longtime clerk in Scott County," the article noted, said, "'Look at my boy right there. He's got a snake under his cap.'" The men did not harm the snakes. They turned them loose soon after catching them. The men simply enjoyed each other's company, and I envied them. Men's jaunts have disappeared from my part of Connecticut. Certainly I've never heard of any snake-handling clubs. As I read the article, I wondered if I could join the group as a member in absentia. Each spring I catch snakes. I'm careful not to hurt them. I have never put one under a cap, but I have dropped a score down my shirt, and once when Eliza was little, I put a small red-bellied snake in my mouth and asked her to kiss me.

I answered Jimmy's letter immediately. I said that I was so busy going to concerts and art galleries that a snake couldn't find a cracked minute through which it could slither into my consciousness. Still I asked, "Is what I heard about the wife of the governor of Mississippi true?" According to a rumor rife in Democratic circles, the governor's wife was slightly addicted to alcohol. One evening she supposedly barged into a tavern on the outskirts of Jackson and demanded a bottle of bourbon even though she didn't have any money in her purse. When the bartender asked why she wanted the whiskey, she said that a rattlesnake had bitten the governor and she needed the whiskey to save his life. "Was the snake big?" the bartender asked. "Big!" she shouted, stretching her arms wide, "why that snake was as long as a well rope, and once it took holt, it pretty near chawed my old man's foot off."

In *Mrs. Appleyard's Year* (1941), the heroine mulled making New Year's resolutions. Since Mrs. Appleyard, Louise Andrews Kent wrote, "has had most of her defects for over half a century, she is well acquainted with them. Some of them, indeed, have become enjoyable simply because she has had them so long." I have similarly grown accustomed to and easy with my faults, though I have lived with my failings longer than Mrs. Appleyard lived with hers. Occasionally I contemplate stripping long-eared tales from my pages, leaving my paragraphs to flow with the milk and honey of thought and description. Such a winnowing, though, is impossible. Where there is milk, there are cows, and where there are cows, there is, thank goodness, manure.

Life is a tangled thread. Rarely have I spent midsummer in Connecticut. On the first of July, I pushed medical matters and their palliative accompaniment, medicinal story, from mind. The proper study of July is July. In June rain had fallen in smothering, mildewing blankets. Woods swelled luxuriant and primeval, partridge berry creeping in capillaries across the ground and Indian pipes rising in choruses of white organs. Vireos called, the sound like faucets endlessly dripping. Petals fell from catalpa flowers and formed loose white mounds on the shoulders of roads. Daylilies turned drainage ditches orange and spiked. Satchels of seeds hung from hop hornbeam, and perfume from lindens eddied across the university grounds, slowing passersby.

Although I did not see anything I hadn't noticed before, the season seemed new. Perhaps the operation I had in early June and its attendant thoughts of jabbing and sawing intensified the pleasures of July, if not of my observations. Instead of learning new tricks, aging canines sometimes so appreciate the old that it seems almost new. Be that as it may, I lingered in field and forest. An osprey slid through an arc above the beaver meadow. Flowers dangled from privet in streams of white tears, and milkweed buds bobbled into bloom. Sealed to the upper surfaces of witch hazel leaves were carpenter shops of tacklike galls. Water snakes wrinkled around the sedges in the beaver pond, and red-winged blackbirds called from alders. Bird's-foot trefoil glowed buttery amid crown vetch, this last white and purple and bumbling with bees. Daisy fleabane stood tall above the meadow, its small flowers fostering an impression of enervation, caused perhaps by a debilitating spring fever. I watched dragonflies: darners flying rhomboids high in the air; near the ground clubtails, their wings gossamer, abdomens yellow in the sunlight; then, clinging to tussock sedges, my favorites, spangled skimmers, thoraxes and abdomens, blue as evening, stigmas on their wings eyelids of black and white, the black near the tips of the insect's wing, the white closer to the body— dragonflies that belonged in *The Book of Beauty,* I told Vicki.

Early in July my blood was tested to see if my thyroid was percolating normally. It wasn't. But I did not tell Vicki, and instead of waiting a fortnight and enduring another round of tests as a doctor advised, I booked passage on the ferry sailing from Bar Harbor to Yarmouth. "Knowing that everything to do with your operation is over must make you feel good," Vicki said. "Yep," I answered, thinking about the marsh hawks that soared over the blueberry field in Nova Scotia, under them altars yellow with swamp candles. I told Vicki I'd been thinking about a tourist who visited the agricultural exhibition in Yarmouth last summer. "Heavens," he exclaimed, when he saw a monstrously big hog. "How many hams can you get out of a beast like that?" "Great god," Vicki said. "You could put Argus to sleep." "Oh," I responded, "that reminds me of a news item Josh told me about." A sheriff in Tupelo, Mississippi, discovered a sleepwalker wandering the downtown, "near the A&W Root Beer stand as I recall." The man only wore an undershirt, one so short that it barely covered his organs of generation. "I'm a somnambulist," the man explained after the sheriff woke him up. "I don't care a hoot in hell about your religion," the sheriff responded. "For all I care you could be a Thirty-second Degree Lumbee and have a B.A. from the College of Cardinals in Rome, Italy. All I know is that if you're going to stroll around Tupelo at night, you are going to have to wear trousers."

Everything Can't
Be Perfect

One mild fall evening a farmer and his wife sat on the front porch rocking. Dinner had been good: chicken that pecked through bushels of bugs to sweetness, turnip greens seasoned by hog not worms, blood-red tomatoes, and rolls rounder than the harvest moon. The mortgage had been paid off. Bobwhites were whistling. Corn was in the crib; tobacco in the barn, and in the pasture cattle were fatter than alfalfa. "All this," the farmer mused, sweeping his right arm through a semicircle, "the crops, the fields, all this don't leave much to ask for." "Yes," his wife answered, pausing and glancing toward the glow coming from a town over a nearby ridge, "if it weren't for our two daughters lying over yonder in the graveyard, everything would be perfect." When his wife stopped talking, the farmer stared dolefully at his calloused hands. "Maw," he said eventually, picking at a cuticle of dirt on his left thumb, "Maw, I know I shouldn't ought to say any such of a thing, but sometimes I wishes they was dead."

This summer Vicki and I left for Nova Scotia in mid-July, later than usual in hopes of avoiding the summer monsoon with its squalls of ticks and blackflies. Memories are brief. The anticipation of difference pushes the actual from recollection. Vicki records each summer's weather on a calendar. The day we arrived in Beaver River was overcast, and that night I studied last year's calendar. During July only five days had been sunny. The pattern continued until our departure on August 24 with eighteen of the days in August foggy or rainy. "At least the blackflies are gone," I said to Vicki. "But not the ticks," she said, plucking two off her trousers.

Despite three decades of experience to the contrary, I dreamed of dozing through the summer, having repressed memories of the two weeks always necessary to settling into place. Sheets covered furniture, turning the house into a succession of ghost rooms. Downstairs spare shutters leaned against windowpanes, blocking sunlight, twine keeping them from slipping loose and falling onto the floor. Tacked over the upstairs windows were squares of brown paper. Screens stood close by against walls. Fixing them into place was always bruising as mildew locked the sashes tight onto sills. To prevent light from shining through the upper portions of windows and rinsing boards blond, stacks of newspapers covered floors. Sealing the side and front doors were homemade storm doors constructed from heavy slabs of wood bolted together. Vicki and I had to disassemble the doors and carry them into the barn in pieces. Setting our mailbox in place on the shoulder of Route 1 necessitated pounding a crowbar deep through topsoil into clay, the crowbar seeming heavier each summer. Advertising flyers were the only mail we received. Still, the day after arriving, I fixed the mailbox on the road, just in case, I said to Vicki, "we receive a letter." For the same contingent feeling, rather than reason, we had the telephone connected although fund-raisers for a police charity were the only people, aside from our children, who called during the three months we were in Canada.

On arriving, I had to relearn rituals that I forgot each year, those, for example, associated with operating the wood stove, not simply splitting logs into the correct size but of sliding levers and twisting knobs, opening the flue and emptying the firebox, this last always on Wednesdays and Sundays. Putting the house into livable shape was a chore that never ended: beating rugs, dusting, sweeping then unpacking the two storerooms that contained gable clocks, oil paintings, and kitchen and decorative ware, these last including diminutive dories and hand-carved wooden figures, among them, lumbermen, oxen hauling carts, horses pulling logs, pickings from sixty-two years of sales, things that furnish memories and musty rooms, making living joyous.

June is blooming month. By the time of our arrival, the rugosa roses in the side yard had blown. Pods had swollen green on blue flag, and dame's rocket had shrunk into spindles of stems and propeller-like leaves. Lupine had disappeared from roadsides, and the sconces of blossoms on horse chestnuts had dried to knobby wicks. Although summer's blooming doesn't collapse until fall, its great milky profusion had curdled inward toward seed. Minute flowers speckled winterberry, at first glance looking like lichens shredded by storms. Along the bluff overlooking the Gulf of Maine, cat's ears were yellow, and ribbons of wild radish waved amid rocks above high tide. June is also growing month. In previous summers I pulled and trimmed before Virginia creeper spooled through the roses and before knotweed spread into thick clumps, its leaves broad spatulas, sliding under the sunlight causing plants below to wither into compost. By the time I began gardening, the stems of dock were thick as fingers and the vines of bittersweet nightshade had tied themselves into curtains. During winter a thunderous wind had blown through the spruce south of the house, toppling and shattering scores of trees. Roots of spruce run broad and shallow rather than deep, and when the trees blow over, the roots pull up oblong lids of dirt and moss. One of the lids I measured was sixteen feet tall and eighteen wide. The trees obliterated old paths while simultaneously opening the woods to colonizers, shanks of blackberry and raspberry canes, rowels rolling sharp about them. For eleven of our first fourteen days in Nova Scotia, the rain fell hard as Sheetrock. Between storms I blazed new paths around briar patches and rails of trees, always getting soaked by sudden downpours, my socks never dry.

When I groused, Vicki said that work got me out of the house and "out of my way," adding, "What else are you going to do? You have read all the books in the Yarmouth library." Not every book, but, alas, in previous summers I read five of the first eight books I borrowed, the discoveries usually coming late in the afternoon after I settled into a soft chair in the study, a pot of warming Scottish breakfast tea on the table to my right. Books are a big part of summers in Nova Scotia. I have written one or two in the study, but usually I read or buy them, this last at the Yarmouth County Museum sale, the price fifty cents for a hardback, though this year a slow boy manning the stall mistakenly charged me a dollar for one volume. Complaining about half a dollar would have made me appear ridiculous. Still the error so irritated me beyond common sense that I wondered if I was losing my reason.

At the sale I bought three books. I considered buying others, some primarily for their titles, for example, Michael Sadleir's novel *Fanny by Gaslight* and Norman Vincent Peale's *Stay Alive All Your Life*. "What else can you do, even if both you and your family wish you were dead?" a man slightly older than me and leaning on a metal hospital cane said on noticing the title. The first paragraph of Albert Payson Terhune's dog story *Lad* stated, "Lady was as much a part of Lad's everyday life as the sunshine itself. She seemed to him quite as perfect, and as gloriously indispensable." Vicki did not quite measure up to Lady. She was as much a part of my Canadian life as the weather, not as sunshine, however, for she was inclined to scold, but as rain. Nevertheless she was indispensable, keeping me fed, clothed, and entertained. "In any case," I thought, placing *Lad* back among the books for sale, "everything can't be perfect."

I bought Alice Caldwell Hegan's *Mrs. Wiggs of the Cabbage Patch* (1901), a book Mother once said was a childhood favorite, along with Frances Hodgson Burnett's *Racketty-Packetty House* (1906) and *Miss Minerva and William Green Hill* (1909) by Frances Boyd Calhoun. Mrs. Wiggs, the novel began promisingly, "was a philosopher, and the sum and substance of her philosophy lay in keeping the dust off her rose-colored spectacles. When Mr. Wiggs traveled to eternity by way of the alcohol route, she buried his faults with him and for want of better virtues to extol she always laid stress on the fine hand he wrote. It was the same way when their little country house burned and she had to come to the city to seek work; her one comment was: 'Thank God, it was the pig instid of the baby that was burned.'" Unfortunately after its lively start the story drifted downward becoming an account of virtuous poverty rewarded with a love story for a subplot, a narrative that would have appealed to Mother when she was a little girl but not as much to me, aging, rain weary, and muscle sore from sawing fallen spruce. I learned, however, that the phrase "came from the Cabbage Patch," something I'd heard when I was a child and living in a more structured society, meant that someone grew up poor.

In 1902 "Will" inscribed my copy of *Mrs. Wiggs*, giving it to "Joe." For Christmas 1918, Cecile M. Burrell received Marjorie Benton Cooke's *Bambi*, the second book I bought. "Bambi," the puff on the book jacket claimed, was "the gayest, cleverest, most scintillating piece of romantic comedy that has come the way of a publishing house in many months." Bambi appeared on the cover wearing a loose shift and leaning forward, eyes glazed and blue, lips full and red, nothing like the ingenue who was the heroine of the novel. I was tired of girls being named Laquisha and Torquemada, I explained to the woman manning the stall when I bought the book, adding that the time was ripe to return to solid WASP names like Bambi and Snookums. Alas, on reading the novel, I learned that Bambi was simply a fond diminutive of Bambina, the nickname of Francesca Parkhurst, the daughter of Professor James Parkhurst.

The last book I bought was E. Phillips Oppenheim's *Exit a Dictator*, a thriller describing the overthrow of Stalin by Alexander, a distant sprig of the Romanoff family. Stalin was banished to Georgia, and the revolution was bloodless, packing cathedrals and churches "with sobbing multitudes" and to the streets bringing "crowds hysterical with joy" and singing "ancient hymns." *Exit a Dictator* appeared in 1939, clearly before Germany invaded Poland, starting World War II. My copy had once belonged to the library at the Royal Canadian Air Force station at

Dartmouth. A sticker pasted to the binding of the book urged borrowers to "treat this book as your own, so that others may benefit from it." The novel was popular in 1944, being checked out seven times from April through October. In 1950 the book was checked out once after which the record stopped. Some of Oppenheim's spy novels crackled. *Exit* fizzled, the prose damp, the women almost always "radiant," the villains cartoonish, one having a "long scraggily neck," "calculating mouth," and "ferret-like eyes." The other villain was "a thickset, burly man, with close-cropped black hair," "a heavy jowl," and "small inset eyes." When the veins stretching like pipes across his protruding forehead swelled, the man's eyes gleamed cruelly, turning him into a fairy-tale ogre.

I forget the well made while I remember the oddities of lesser books, the names of Mrs. Wiggs's daughters, for example, Asia, Australia, and Europena. The rough hewn and flawed attract me. "The air is so fresh that sleep must come easily and last long in Nova Scotia," an acquaintance said before I left Connecticut. No, early in the morning red squirrels racketed through the walls, waking me and the dogs. Before putting the dogs outside, I mulled oddity, fictional doings suitable to the dozy moments of half-thought: the girl who ate so much seafood doused with antibiotics on fish farms that her boyfriend became allergic to her, breaking out in hives after holding her hand and, once, after kissing her almost dying from toxic shock. I often thought about diet. One morning I pondered the case of a woman who ate so many vegetables slathered with pesticides that she gave birth to a six-legged infant. Once free from its cocoon the child contracted its mandibles and pinched the midwife, causing her to fling her forceps against a wall and jitterbug out of the room. The baby then hopped onto the floor and scuttled out the door and down the hall, its escape from the maternity ward prevented by its being netted by an entomologist visiting his wife, hospitalized after a recent visit to Africa, suffering from an infestation of Tumbu fly maggots. "My God," a pediatrician exclaimed after learning about the birth, "buying shoes will bankrupt those poor parents." Weather as much as the half-light of morning may have been responsible for my thinking such things. Some days the wind was so strong that I could not look straight ahead. The wind bent vision, blowing it into a curve, so that I saw only what was beside me or around a nearby corner. As my vision went, so perhaps did thought, spinning dizzily, rolling over one roundabout after another.

Making things perfect strips the quick from life, flattening both sadness and humor. The curator of the Yarmouth County Museum furnished a room like a doctor's office, most of the appointments dating from 1870 to 1910. On the wall hung a bronze plate reading, "Dr. C. A. Webster Office Hours, 12–2 P.M. and 6–8 P.M." Suspended above the plate was a parchment dated 1857 and testifying that John R. Webster "has attended the practice of Medical and Surgical wards of Bellevue Hospital for the term of six months." On the certificate appeared Bellevue Hospital, the building not symmetrical but nevertheless balanced, the main section five stories high and topped by a cupola, the two wings, each four stories, to the right side a smaller, three-story building, home perhaps to an admitting office or wards for virulent diseases. On a shelf in the room stood a wooden pestle and mortar and a ceramic container shaped like an urn, eight inches tall and four and a half wide, the top looking like a saltshaker pitted with holes. Printed on the bowl of the urn in gold letters was the word *Leeches*. Beside the urn was a medical kit, three bottles and forty-four containers resembling test tubes filling it like cells in a beehive, all the cells sealed by stoppers. A miscellany of material filled the tubes: cascara compound no. 3, digitalis tincture, Dover's powder, potassium arsenite solution, and a blend of calomel, ipecac, and sodium bicarbonate, among a pharmacy of others.

Above the doctor's rolltop desk was a shelf of books, affirming my faith in the waggish, creative nature of human beings strong enough to resist the temptation of perfection. Most of the books were conventional nineteenth-century medical manuals: Bryant's *Practice of Surgery, Diseases of the Chest and the Principles of Physical Diagnosis* by Norris and Landis, Hartley's *Medical Chemistry*, and C. H. Cleaveland's *Medical Pronouncing Lexicon*. Leaning against *Uterine Versions and Flexions* was, however, *The Illustrated Horse Doctor* by Mayhew. Under the title on the spine of the book appeared an illustration, a horse standing under a tree, a rail fence behind him, and checkered blanket draped over his loins and hind quarters. I studied the office. Nothing else was out of place. The book was tincture enough, though, to make me smile, if not snort in pleasure. Of course treatments prescribed for horses were often similar to those applied to people. In a chapter entitled "The Annexation of Cuby," the name appropriated from geographical Cuba, Mrs. Wiggs's son Billy persuaded the owner of an ancient horse that was "most gone" to give him the animal rather than shoot it. Mrs. Wiggs's treatment saved the animal from the knackers. She stuffed a calomel pill wrapped in "soft, light bread" into the horse's mouth washing it down the animal's throat with a tonic composed of water and turpentine. The dose helped, but afterward Mrs. Wiggs realized that "violent measures were necessary," for "the old horse had evidently seen a vision of the happy hunting-ground, and was loath to return to the sordid earth." She bound a rag carpet around the horse's middle, forced its hooves onto hot tallow, and chased the tonic with the family dinner, a kettle of soup to which she added so much pepper that the horse would "think he's having a sun-stroke." The ministrations succeeded, and Cuby became a working member of the Wiggs household, pulling a cart from the back of which Billy sold kindling.

Discovering the *Horse Doctor* so invigorated me that on the drive back to Beaver River from Yarmouth, Vicki and I stopped at the Quick 'n' Tasty for pie and coffee. Vicki ordered blueberry pie, and I, coconut cream. My piece was every boy's dream, the filling chewy and yellow, the meringue wind blown with coconut, the whole massive, seven and a half inches wide at the round part of the crust. "Can you eat all that?" Vicki asked. "Watch," I said. I became a sight that "sored" eyes. Before I finished the pie, I longed for a tumbler of Mrs. Wiggs's tonic. Instead of eating, I was "jes chawing," as Billy described attempting to eat all of a big meal. "The slice looked perfect," Vicki said as we walked back to the car. "Perfection isn't everything," I said. "The next time I want a piece that is a little flawed, one that leaves me dissatisfied, alert, and thinking I did not get my money's worth."

Plots

One Sunday afternoon near the end of July, Vicki and I visited four gardens in Yarmouth. For forty years owners had dug and filled, transforming spruce thickets and the corners of pastures bristly with alders into small plots of order and beauty. Daylilies shined brassy, their petals practically notes, usually orange and yellow but occasionally scarlet. Astilbe was misty and demure. Goatsbeard dangled leeringly; the canes of rambling roses tumbled akimbo, and Japanese iris spread baked into blue and white, the season's horticultural willow pattern. Along a path pieris flowers had folded into small seed purses, but Siebold's magnolia still bloomed. Never before had I seen the magnolia. The flowers were white cream pitchers, the petals sides of the bowl, at the bottom pink stamens swirling around a yellow cone.

Gardening is a difficult and an almost moral activity. Living is easier if one eschews trowels and beliefs and allows life to meander a weedy course. Of course the hankering for order can rage virulent and, like pesticides, can blister and burn away the random and unexpected, depriving society of vitality. Beyond beds and paths hours sprawl into the random, refusing attempts to clip them and arrange them in vases or, in the case of writing, force them into paragraphs. On the other hand the gardens Vicki and I explored had not been chopped sterile into straight and narrow gates but were oases, offering respite, cooling life's hot incessant fret. In contrast most of the days and plots I wander are overgrown, rhizomes pushing up the unexpected, more often than not intriguing rather than upsetting me, reflecting my character more than anything else.

The agricultural portion of the Southwestern Nova Scotia Exhibition has withered, the hatchery, for example, once squawking with chickens reduced to single cage in the "Kiddie Barn." Consequently this summer I wandered the midway. At the Truck Stop, a train of six small tractors rode a railed highway. The tractors were different colors: black, green, pink, white, red, and orange. Two children sat in each cab, one turning a plastic wheel, the other, a brother or sister hitchhiking along for the ride. Teenagers lined up for the Tilt-A-Whirl. Around and rising above riders buckled into seats were pink and yellow metal scallop shells, their shape reminding me of high-backed rattan Victorian porch chairs. Once the ride began, the shells shook back and forth and spun around, the sight so dizzying me that I could not watch. More to my liking was Bear Affair, large plastic bears sitting on their haunches, their stomachs dens in which small children sat with a parent. The bears had names, and I wrote them down as they revolved slowly along a track: Buzz, Lally, Bucky, and Bloake. A man overseeing a dry pond filled with small metallic frogs noticed me. Punters fished for the frogs, using poles baited with magnets. Stamped on the underside of each frog was a number, and if a fisherman was lucky, he gigged a prize, the best being a stuffed bear. The man asked why I was jotting down notes. Before I answered, he described his job and the long hours necessary to erect the midway. In the past carnival work was seasonal, and sometimes employees were rough hewn. I told him about a visit I made several years ago to the Woodstock Fair in Connecticut in which several workers were doped beyond lethargy, the sounds coming from their mouths not words but syllables, one ride on a Ferris wheel lasting two minutes, the next fourteen. "Today that would not happen," the man said, "somebody could get killed." I glanced at the octopus-like Scrambler, its long arms revolving, the compartments at their ends spinning, almost sizzling. "A ride in one of those compartments would kill me," I said and walked away.

Occasionally this summer I occupied an actual plot. Opposite the cash registers in Sobey's Grocery is "Geezer Corner," as Vicki dubbed it. To free themselves to putter aisles, wives park aging husbands in the corner. Three weeks ago Vicki bought an egg-salad sandwich at the food counter, giving me half when she dumped me in the corner. The sandwich was good. I fell asleep after eating, and shopping passed satisfactorily and comfortably for both Vicki and me.

The dreams of youth are expansive. They spread beyond the immediate, stretching over wood and pasture. Contemplating them requires sheds of costly equipment: cultivators, tuition for graduate studies, harvesters, and muscular naïveté enough to plow doubt out of mind. Time inevitably tosses reason into the mental works, and most people eventually become minimalists, avoiding scramblers, both mechanical and intellectual. Instead they cultivate small plots, their sight focused on the particular, not the romantic, which is often so vague that leaf and stem vanish into nothingness. The first evening in Nova Scotia I mowed grass that had grown over the grave of George, a dachshund I buried under a willow at the edge of the side meadow three years ago. The mower I pushed was over eighty years old, the clacking of the blades not cacophonous but in tune with moody evening, the sun out of sight below the Gulf of Maine, red and orange having leached out of the sky, leaving timbres of gray and blackening blue behind, here and there splinters of silver. The next week Vicki turned the grave into a whirligig garden, planting four plastic daisies beside the grave. The daisies' petals were various colors, green, yellow, red, and blue, and spun in the wind. In the ground at the foot of the grave Vicki stuck two purchases from the Dollar Store, a humming-bird with a green body and purple tail and a chartreuse dragonfly. Both creatures were plastic, and their wings also spun in the breeze.

Dogs are aging people's toys. A few are big and shaggy, resembling stuffed animals given as prizes at carnivals. Most older people who own dogs, though, have little dogs, dolls like George, initially purchased for children but becoming theirs after children grow up and decamp. Vicki and I now own three small dogs, two of them registered mongrels, Suzy, a Greater Hartford Street Mongrel, and Jack, a Lesser Madisonville, Ten-nessee, Kill-Shelter Mongrel. Penny, the third dog, came from a puppy mill. She weights eight pounds. Her hearing is bad; she is almost blind. She leans to the right and staggers when she walks. Warts pepper her, and her coat is scuffed. Bare patches the size of eggs have hatched on her flanks, and she stinks, no bath strong enough to eradicate the stench of rotting age. Yet because she had been ours for fifteen years we nursed her in Nova Scotia, her needs an enclosure that penned us to house and schedule. No longer could she navigate stairs. At midnight Vicki brought her upstairs and tucked her into her pod, a small cloth basket with high, rounded sides that press against and reassure her. At 6:15 I carried her downstairs. The stairway consisted of fourteen steps. I cradled Penny against my left side. Because I was not as steady on my feet as I once was, my right leg having suddenly weakened, I seized the banister with my right hand. Penny couldn't manage the three steps leading from the side porch into the yard, so I carried her into the grass, the dew always soaking my slippers. After she pumped herself dry, I lifted her and took her into the kitchen where she crawled into another small bed and fell asleep. For my part I was awake, and I did morning chores. I emptied the slop bucket into the meadowsweet across the yard and brought wood in from the barn and laid a fire in the stove. By the time I finished eat-ing breakfast, Penny was awake. She stumbled out of the bed and put a paw on my foot, a sign that she needed to go outside again. Throughout the day I transported Penny in and out of the house, fourteen times being the norm. "When we are old," Vicki asked last week, "do you think the children will take such good care of us?" "No," I said, pausing, bile suddenly boiling, "and I don't give a damn."

In Nova Scotia many creatures besides dogs interested me. This summer tachinid flies seemed everywhere. Along the lane to the bluff overlooking the Gulf of Maine, the leaves of alder, wild raisin, bay, and winterberry bristled with flies. To control gypsy moth caterpillars, a tachinid, *Compsilura concinnata,* was introduced into the northeast without determining beforehand if the fly would parasitize the caterpillars of any of the two hundred or so native moths and butterflies. During July I saw few moths. For the past few years I have seen almost no large sphinx moths, and I wonder if *Compsilura concinnata* is responsible for the dearth. As a family tachinids are efficient predators. Some lay eggs directly on host insects. Others insert eggs into prey. Some species attack hard-shelled insects using piercing devices that look like beer-can openers, church keys, while still others lay eggs in places where prey are likely to appear. During summer I read libraries of butchery novels in which heroes and villains plot ways to prey upon or protect host populations. Their machinations are rarely as ingenious as those of insects. Some phorid, or scuttle, flies are known as ant-decapitating flies. A female phorid inserts her egg into a carpenter ant. After hatching, the maggot dines on the innards of the ant. Eventually the maggot hollows out the ant's head, devouring the contents, after which it produces an enzyme that severs the tissue attaching the head to the rest of the ant's body. The head breaks free, and the maggot pupates within the shell or snuggery, as I prefer to think it. "We need a plague of the flies in Storrs. They'd kill the carpenter ants that spill out of our house every spring," Vicki said after I described the ant decapitator.

At dusk, midges, probably male chironomids, often swarmed in the side yard. When I stood on the well cover, a swarm gathered, twirling above my head. If I raised an arm, the swarm wheeled upward and splattered outward into loose streamers of dark dots. When I lowered my arm, the swarm pulled back together, tightening into a flimsy hairnet above my head. If I moved across the yard, the swarm accompanied me, its current, meandering or frenetic, reacting to my motion, making me smile and sometimes laugh aloud.

The warblers and plovers that forage wood and shore respectively did not appear this summer. For several years their numbers have decreased, and I wondered if bird life had sunk into such an absence that only emptiness could follow. Nonetheless hummingbirds zithered about the house. One afternoon I relieved myself near a rhododendron white with late blossoms. Sunlight made my urine sparkle. The glitter and perhaps sugar attracted a ruby-throated hummingbird, a female bustling about the rhododendron. The bird jittered back and forth, less than an inch away, its green back golden in the light. I remained motionless observing the bird until it floated upward too close to petal and stamen, and I shooed it away. Several times since, I have "baited" hummingbirds, but they have not risen to the chum, something that reassures me as sugar in one's urine is more a medical than an ornithological matter.

In mid-July a circle of swamp candles bloomed in the blueberry field. The diameter of the circle was thirty-one paces. One morning I stood amid the candles, yellow spires flickering about me. The moment did not inspire; instead it exhilarated. At the edge of the field a hem of fog lingered, veiling a wall of winterberry. If major western religions had evolved amid fog, they'd be less dogmatic. The hard, clear light of the desert contributed to the delusion that man can see and understand. The holy ghost of fog fosters awareness of unknowing, the basis of humility. Inspiration blinds, and what a person should hope for from the natural world is exhilaration, spots of time from which time vanishes—flourishing moments ripe with particular sights, say, of yellow wart mushrooms on a mound of starry moss, the mushrooms four inches tall, their stems bows of white and yellow, their caps orange, on the ground surrounding the moss rails of broken spruce, sleeves of silver and black lichens wrapping them; or six New England asters blooming in a seam of forest, old man's beard greening stunted trees, circling the trees and flowers a collar of cinnamon ferns five feet high; or perhaps simply a glimpse of bullhead lilies in a stream brown with humic acid, the yellow bulbs tricking one into seeing golden filaments wavering under the water.

Such moments linger and often influence action more than long hours of study. The Manor Inn, once a sea captain's home, closed this year, and Vicki and I spent a Saturday at the inn's going-out-of-business sale. Mahogany doors were priced at $400, stainless steel bowls at $10 and $15. Four poster beds were marked $1,000, while tourist bicycles with fat tires were $50. After roaming the inn and wondering who would pay $1,750 for a hot tub on a second floor and almost coveting a television priced at $75, we walked into the rose garden. Once circular, the garden had rambled into weeds and out of definition. In the center was a stagnant pool. In it a single water lily bloomed, two green frogs hunkering close by, practically petals. The roses themselves had sunk out of shape like trash tossed onto a tip. The plants were, however, old-fashioned standbys, and a few canes had sprayed into blossoms. I snapped two of the canes and taking them back to Beaver River planted them alongside the kitchen porch. The roses on both canes were the size of demitasse cups. The flowers on one cane were white; on the other, my favorite, the flowers were pink and sugary, tinged with orange.

Years ago I stopped reading systematically. Twice a week every summer, I borrow a bag of books from the Yarmouth Library. Once back at Four Winds, I invariably discover that I've read two of the books, while another three prove unreadable. Consequently I reread books scattered through the house, always P. G. Wodehouse's *Uncle Fred in the Springtime* and my favorite science fiction novel, *The Day of the Triffids* by John Wyndham. To have written either of the books would have been writing career enough. How marvelous to have frequented Wodehouse's Drones Club in pepperish days when one's appetite for the absurd "what ho" of life was gluttonous. In later years, when the failures of scalpels become staples of conversation, the absurd doesn't spring so nimbly to mind, and readers jettison the jovial for the sensational, becoming devotees of mystery and butchery.

Among the batch of books I borrowed last Friday, four proved unreadable and three were mysteries of sorts, Robert Crais's *Demolition Angel,* the heroine of which belonged to the Los Angeles bomb squad; Bill Pronzini's *Fever,* detailing an adventure of Nameless, Pronzini's detective; and Susan Hill's *The Risk of Darkness,* her Inspector Serrailler one of the tribe of sensitive policemen who have a second, submerged artistic life. The last volume I checked out was *The Wasp Factory,* Iain Banks's first novel, published in 1984 and for me a hilarious shaggy-dog story, not a judgment with which all readers agree, a reviewer in the *Sunday Express* calling the book, "a silly, gloatingly sadistic and grisly yarn of a family of Scots lunatics." Because of something nasty in a ward for deformed children, the hero's older brother abandoned his medical studies and became an arsonist, usually burning pet dogs but occasionally ambling afield, literally, to set flocks of sheep aflame. For his part, after an unfortunate accident, Frank, the main character, embraced murder, knocking off three people before reaching puberty. He insinuated an adder into the artificial leg of his cousin Blyth. Next he convinced his younger brother Paul that a bomb suddenly exposed on a beach by a storm was a bell, the ringing of which would be memorable. Lastly he built a huge kite to which he attached his sweet cousin Esmerelda, sending her over the North Sea to the Great Beyond. "I would like to think," Frank mused, "that she died still being floated by the giant kite, that she went round the world and rose higher as she died of starvation and dehydration and so grew less weighty still, to become eventually, a tiny skeleton riding the jet streams of the planet; a sort of FLYING DUTCH-WOMAN."

The paragraph brought to mind the beginning of Kaye Gibbons's *Ellen Foster,* another book I reread during summer. "When I was little I would think of ways to kill my daddy. I would figure out this or that way and run it down through my head until it got easy," Ellen recounted. "The way I liked best was letting go a poisonous spider in his bed. It would bite him and he'd be dead and swollen up and I would shudder to find him so. Of course I would call the rescue squad and tell them to come quick something's the matter with my daddy. When they come in the house I'm all in a state of shock and just don't know how to act what with two colored boys just heaving my dead daddy onto a roller cot. I just stand in the door and look like I'm shaking all over."

The books I borrowed filled the scuttles of empty afternoons. Rarely did they make me smile. Once in a while, though, I stumbled across an old tale told to vary narrative pace. A farmer, I read, fell behind in paying for his subscription to a newspaper, say the *Nashville Tennessean.* When he wrote the editor explaining that he had no money, the editor replied, saying that the next time the farmer was in Nashville, he could bring two or three bushels of corn to the his office. "That will settle the bill." "Great god!" the farmer answered, "if I had any corn then I'd have some cobs, and if I had cobs, why would I want your damned old paper?"

Fog limits vision to the immediate. Early in August, Vicki and I drove to Gateway Park in South Yarmouth and watched the finals of the Canadian National Oldtimers Baseball Championship, the thirty-five-and-over division, pitting Yarmouth's Red Knights against a team from Ontario, the Tillsonburg Old Sox. Vicki packed potato chips, olives, radishes, carrots, and slices of chocolate cake, and we stopped at Little Lebanon and picked up pita sandwiches bulging with tomatoes, lettuce, tahini sauce and kibbe. Three hundred people watched the game, a huge crowd for Yarmouth. Fog was thick, and from the stands the field was almost opaque. Every time a player hit a pop fly, the ball vanished from my sight, though not always from the sight of outfielders, two of Yarmouth's being lobstermen accustomed to finding pots, if not baseballs, in heavy fog. Vicki and I sat along the third-base line on the fourth row of the grandstand, there being only six rows. The man in front of me was also a lobsterman. "I catch them, but I won't eat them," he said, adding "ugh" for emphasis. Next to him sat a burly man who had won two 50-50s in December, $1,800 that he used to repair "the old Ford." Tickets for 50-50s are sold at many sporting events in Nova Scotia. Tickets usually cost a dollar, the winner splitting the proceeds with a charity.

Mounted on the home plate screen high behind the catcher were two metal signs, one with an eight printed on it, the other with a nine, the first being the number of a pitcher who had a heart attack and died on the mound during a game, the second the number of a player killed in a car wreck while driving home after a game. Rules of the Oldtimers game differed from those of conventional baseball. A team was not allowed to score more than six runs in an inning, the exception being the final inning. If a team was behind by ten runs at the end of the fifth inning, a "mercy" rule ended the game. If a catcher was a base runner, as soon as his team made its second out, a pinch runner replaced him so he could don his gear and be ready to catch at the end of his team's at bats. Games lasted seven innings unless they went into extra innings. With the exception of the final pitcher who was allowed to pitch three innings and if need be additional innings, pitchers could only pitch for two innings. Thus a team's first pitcher handled the initial two innings, and a second pitcher innings three and four. "Two innings are enough for our arms," a player from a team eliminated earlier in the tournament said to me. Many players were graying and hefty and lumbered the base paths, making me feel comfortable, recollections of vanished youth never percolating wistfully into mind. The game began poorly for the Red Knights as Tillsonburg's leadoff batter hit a home run. In the second inning, however, errors helped Yarmouth bound ahead. The Knights kept the lead and won, 7–3, in regulation, a result that satisfied spectators, many of whom were my age and who, if they resembled me, had begun to suffer back pains in the fourth inning, the ratcheting sort of ache that makes people neglect batters, not a good thing, especially if they sat along the third base line in, as it was called, "the dentist's waiting room."

Many Americans only have institutional educations in common, wealth having created the suburb and fostered mobility, in the process undermining community and loyalty to place. As a consequence many people know their fellow college alumni better than their neighbors. Nova Scotia's French coast runs from Beaver River along the Bay of Fundy north to Weymouth on Route 1 and has been called the longest main street in North America. The administrative district is called Clare. For a fortnight each summer the Clare Acadian Festival takes place, this past summer's festival's being the fifty-fourth. The first Sunday in August, Vicki and I drove to Church Point for the festival bazaar held at the University of Saint Anne, the drive taking forty minutes.

Church Point, the university, and the festival are all small plots, focusing attention on the immediate and the communal. A lumberjack competition took place in a parking lot in front of the library. Vicki and I watched several events. In the ax throw, competitors threw a double-edged, medieval-looking ax at a bull's eye. Circles rippled out from the red center of the bull's-eye, white, blue, and white again. Lodging the ax in the red was worth five points, the inner white four, the blue three, and the outer white two pints. Competitors were entitled to four throws, the first, a practice throw. Most grasped the bottom of the ax handle with both hands and swung the ax up and down, practicing their strokes and getting into rhythm. Steve, a block of a man wearing a gray T-shirt with the sleeves hacked off, held the ax only in his right hand. His score was eleven. Winton, a lean man who had aged into the frailty of a sapling, swayed back and forth but scored nine points, one of his throws slipping from the target, the other two a five and a four.

Two-man teams sawed through eight-by-eight beams, the contestants spreading their legs wider than their shoulders, the best teams pulling and pushing in rhythm. In another contest individuals sawed through a beam using a swede, or bow, saw. Lumberjacks also competed using chain saws, the competition consisting of three cuts, the contestants picking saws off the ground at the start of the competition and slicing down, then up, then down again cutting three slabs of wood off the beam. In logrolling the two-man teams used peaveys to turn a log over and back along a course raised on rails, pushing the log up an incline, controlling it while it rolled down the other side to a stop, then reversing direction and pushing it back up the incline and directing it as it rolled back to the start of the course. In the kettle boil two-person teams boiled a can of water, one man shaving cuts from a log using an ax, the other building and managing a fire under the can. The competitors and spectators knew one another. Vicki and I seemed the only outlanders at the competition, not something that was bothersome as chat lodged us in place. Next to us stood a welder who worked in the shipyard at Meteghan. His brother-in-law had just built a house on the Beaver River outlet across a pasture and marsh from our property. "Say hello to him when you see him," the man said.

Craftsmen set up booths in a second parking lot. From a woman from whom she purchased aprons last summer on Water Street in Yarmouth,

Vicki bought two potholders decorated with lighthouses. For lunch we split half a chicken and a six-dollar platter of haddock and fried scallops, the second sold by the Clare Lions, the first from volunteers raising money for the Little Brook Fire Department. The woman who waited on us worked for the tourist office in Yarmouth. She recognized me, and as she handed me our chicken asked, "How is life in Beaver River?" Vicki and I ate in the university gymnasium, paying bingo while we ate, five cards costing a dollar. After lunch I bought a rappie pie from Rapure à Evelina and put it in the car, planning to eat it for dinner the next night. We listened to fiddlers. I recognized some tunes, "Buffalo Gals," for example. I am sucker for weepy tunes, "Lamp Lighting Time in the Valley" being typical. Having left home and wandered the crooked and broad way, the narrator imagined his aged mother lighting a lamp in her window every night, hoping it would guide her wayward son home. "I can see her as she rocks in her chair to and fro," the narrator recounted, determining to change his ways and meet her, not, alas, at their earthly home, but in heaven.

The fair's main event was a parade running two miles from Little Brook along Route 1 until it turned aside ending on the university campus. Police closed the highway, and people set up folding chairs in yards and along both shoulders of the road to watch the parade. Many families raised tents and cooked lunches outside. The oxen and massive workhorses once common at country festivals have disappeared. A tractor pulled a flatbed on the back of which appeared an Acadian family wearing deerskins, the most appealing member of the family an old woman who removed her false teeth and cackled loudly. J. R. Belliveau, an excavator, towed a troop of Boy Scouts and their canoes. The pumper from the Salmon River Fire Department, the department that served Beaver River, blew its siren. A truck pulled a green and yellow John Deere X300 mower, the prize of a raffle to benefit Clare Minor Hockey, a ticket costing ten dollars. College students bobbled past wearing huge papier-mâché heads, holes in the necks enabling students to see where they were walking. Two girls carried an advertising banner, "Live Well With Pharmasave." Seven Mardi Gras figures with orange noses shaped like carrots handed out beaded plastic necklaces. A man rode a penny-farthing, and two men puttered along, each mounted on a homemade "Cow-A-Sockey," a go-cart tinkered into a metallic Holstein, the body of the cow an oil barrel, its head a tire hub, the whole painted black and white. Under the cow's ribs a small motor churned, turning the cow's hooves. Two students juggled yellow balls. Behind them marched a troop of white-haired, often red-faced men wearing capes and caps adorned with ostrich feathers, local Knights of Columbus. In the back of a pickup wallowed a huge potato constructed out of newsprint. Attached to the potato was a sign urging viewers to "Eat Rapure Acadienne." Perched atop the potato was a rooster, the variety bred in a factory manufacturing novelties not a hatchery. "Because Kids Matter to God" declared a poster pasted to the door of another pickup. In the bed of the truck, a dozen children raised and lowered their hands in unison. A sign on the back of the truck read "Awana," beneath which appeared "Cubbies," "Sparks," and "Truth Training," a Bible spread open beside this last phrase. "Oh, dear," Vicki said, as the children raised their arms, "Suffer the little children." "Approved Workers Are Not Ashamed," I replied, quoting 2 Timothy, the first letters of the words spelling Awana, the name of an international evangelical group.

Happily, from my perspective, the parade celebrated this world more than any next: the gustatory pleasures of rappie pie, the muscular joy of canoeing, and sunshine itself, in the light of which beauty queens smiled and waved, from Yarmouth the Seafest Queen and Miss Southwest Nova Scotia. Miss Nova Scotia sat in a chair in the bed of a new blue pickup. Around her ballons bubbled like champagne, red, white, yellow, and purple. "What fun that girl is having," Vicki exclaimed. We, too, had fun, so much so that on the way home we stopped at Comeau's Market in Meteghan Center, and Vicki bought biscuits, a coconut and pineapple tea cake, six chocolate muffins, and five quarts of raspberries. "Beaver River gal, won't you come out tonight," I said scooping up a handful of berries, the taste not just red but a rainbow of colors.

Close Reading

"What's the difference between a flimsy dress and an extracted tooth?" the filler at the bottom of the page asked before answering, "one is *too thin* while the other is *tooth out.*" "Shouldn't a sheep dog have a lamb pup?" another filler mused. Recently I'd read an article praising close observation and criticizing broad generalities. "Long, complex sentences," the article argued, generated elevated thoughts, "thoughts so bloated with helium that they sail out of sight and become invisible and incomprehensible." People would be happier and have "better handles on their lives," the piece stated, if they participated in local, not national, affairs and read regional, not national, newspapers. I decided to test the validity of the article and for the past week have studied two small-town newspapers, the first a local Connecticut paper, the second a paper published in East Tennessee.

For the sake of scientific rigor, I must confess I'm constitutionally inclined toward low not high seriousness, tidbits like the fillers, culled, incidentally, from the paper in Tennessee. Moreover I am not sure what constitutes the great and important, out of necessity leaving me disposed toward the small. These admissions aside, however, reading the papers has entertained, and educated, me. Headlines were endlessly intriguing, "Storrs Man Misses Bus to Hartford," "Bashful Woman with Tiny Head Climbs Ladder," "Dachshund Learns French," and "Female Lunatic Promoted," this last referring to academic doings at the University of Connecticut. The danger, of course, is that close reading so influences the way the reader thinks that he begins to compose his own headlines, many of which feature the unacceptable, phrases such as Ancient Fruit, Fat Betty, and Hung Like a Donkey, or sentences in which Bunions and Prayer and Winkie and Cabbage bump inelegantly against each other. Happily, regional newspapers provide antidotes against unfashionable ponderings. Sometimes a puzzling question diverts thought, one such as

"Have you ever wondered why comets have tails and the dog star does not?" Often a maxim shunts the latent scribbler onto a bucolic siding far from main line of conventional literary genuflection. "The man who sits down on the spur of the moment doesn't sit long," the Connecticut paper declared, the aphorism referring to impressionable people who embrace the au courant.

Both papers printed letters to the editor, the most popular supposedly from children. "I am an orphan and am nine years old," a boy from Niota, Tennessee, wrote. "I live on a farm with my Aunty. Once I lived in town with my mother and father and three sisters and no brothers. But a fire burned our house down. Don't you feel sorry for me, a poor little boy by himself? I like the farm, and I want to plough corn. I have a dog named Psalm. He shakes hands and plays with rabbits and squirrels. I don't like pea pudding. Once my daddy took me to Florida, and I saw a wild yellow pig. Before he burned up, my daddy chewed 8,421 plugs of tobacco and ruined his tummy. Mommy made him take pink pills. When my pet pigeon Esteline got sick, Daddy gave her his pink pills. Daddy did not tell Mommy, and Esteline died. Aunty loves me very much. My birthday is next week, and Aunty is going to give me a canary. She is going to make a chocolate cake, and I will be a happy orphan."

The paper in Tennessee also printed excerpts from novels. *The Mormon Epithalamium* (published 2009) began, "The eleven brides joined the groom at the altar. This was Bascombe's big day. It was also a big day for Toby, Bascombe's ginger-colored dachshund. Toby loved Bascombe and wanted to surprise his master by barking congratulations in French after the ceremony. It was even a big day for Bashful Mary. Although Bascombe was marrying four of her cousins, Mary had not been invited to the wedding. To see the wedding she leaned a ladder against the temple and stuck her small head through a window behind the pews. She heard Toby bark but did not understand his yelps because she assumed he was speaking Spanish."

I did not read more. I have aged into enjoying reading nonfiction more than fiction. I dislike the tension of story, the apprehension awakened by worrying about what will happen next. I prefer the calm of nonfiction. Knowing the ending of a book reduces tension generated by reading and enables me to doze easily into sleep, the book's sliding from my grasp and shutting not making me anxious about losing my place. Writing is, of course, different from reading. The experiences of writing nonfiction and fiction are similar. Unlike a reader, a writer is not at the mercy of a narrative. Instead being bucketed about by tale, he bridles words and steers clear of anxiety. In any case I paid more attention to the nonfiction in the papers than I did to fiction. Under the caption "Incredible Coincidence" appeared the account of a Storrs resident ticketed for speeding late in December. "Mr. Brown [I have changed the name] is 72 years old. This was his first driving infraction, and by an amazing coincidence not once during his entire life had he remarked that he'd never received a speeding ticket."

Both papers published occasional verse. The poetry was the rhyming equivalent of nonfiction, rejecting the imaginary and refusing to transport readers beyond the concrete into a mystifying symbolic landscape in which grasshoppers chewed tobacco and cowboys rode horseradishes. Typical of the newspaper verse were "Roly-Poly" and "Baby Poetry," comfortable poems, the subjects of which were domestic and warmheartedly lactatory.

> As round and plump as a mandarin,
> With a dimpled cheek and a double chin,
> And a mouth just made to keep kisses in,
> Is our little Roly-Poly!
>
> His legs are short, and he stubs his toes,
> And over and over and over he goes,
> But never happens to bump the nose
> Of our little Roly-Poly!

The verse did not soar aloft on "viewless wings," to bring Johnny Keats to mind, though occasionally the spelling was ethereal, particularly in the Tennessee paper.

> Where is the baby! Bess its heart—
> Where is muzzer's darling boy?
> Does it hold its ittle hands apart,
> The dearest, blessed toy?
> And so it does, and will its ittle chin,
> Grow just as fat as butter?
> And will it poke its ittle fingers in
> Its tunnin ittle mouth, and mutter,
> Nicey, wicey words,
> Just like ittle yellow birds?

In addition to the poetic, animal-interest reports enlivened the regional papers. On the outskirts of Cleveland, Tennessee, a slow freight hit a cow, knocking her four yards off the track into a field. Actually the train pushed the cow, for cow landed on her feet and did not appear to be injured. "But didn't the cow look scared afterward?" a reporter asked a farmer who witnessed the accident. "Well," the farmer replied, "I don't know whether she was frightened or not, but she did look a good deal discouraged."

Obituaries marched through the papers in endless columns, some of the accounts so long that they themselves seemed verbal centenarians. When the only Democrat elected to a state judgeship in East Tennessee died in Vonore, his obituary described practically every aspect of life going back to his birth and childhood, even the early days when, to bring the bruised bovine back to mind, the judge was still milking. The judge succumbed to a wasting disease, becoming ill in May and dying hard through June, July, August, and into September. His wife Emma nursed him, and the judge died at home. The ordeal exhausted her, his hacking cough keeping her up at night and, toward the end, corking seepages occupying her days. Not long after the judge's funeral, Emma's friend Normaleen visited her. "Emma didn't look too lively," Normaleen told members of her Parcheesi club. "Of course that's understandable. Between you and me, the Judge has been a mite sight of trouble this summer."

Study of the two papers led me to conclude that celebrating the local and immediate was rational, indeed therapeutic. Accounts in the papers did not make me grind my teeth like prating about athletics and shenanigans in Washington did in national newspapers. Reporters didn't neglect the political, however. The Tennessee paper praised a school board in Loudon County for attempting to weave patriotism into the fabric of the elementary school day. Before beginning tasks, students were required to swear oaths of allegiance. "Do you solemnly swear to support the Constitution of the United States of America, to obey the laws of the Great State of Tennessee, and," the paper reported describing third-grade practice in Madisonville, "to feed Weinie and Tittles our hamsters to the best of your ability, so help you God?"

Paradoxically the only danger was that reading nonfiction stirred the hankering to write fiction. I imagined emending *The Mormon Epithalamium*, reducing the number of Bascombe's wives by ten and turning him into an Episcopalian—not only that, but I would swell the size of Mary's head and invite her to the ceremony, making her a contralto soprano in a cathedral choir. Moreover I'd convert Toby's barks into German, a language I understand, then translate them into English.

Bascombe's remaining bride would be short but lovely. "She would have been taller," Toby barked, raising his right front paw in a canine toast, "but she is made of such precious materials that Nature could not afford to make her larger." In fact after reading the papers, I felt so happy that I was fairly uncomfortable. No matter, if the feeling persisted, all I had to do was buy a bottle Judd's Silver and Gold Magical Elixir, a system renovator and blood purifier, a regimen of which was, an advertisement declared, "guaranteed to warm frosted feet, to strip bark lice from the legs and pluck grubs from the head, to arrest the premature decay of patriotism, to give strength to the weak, money to the poor, boots to the barefoot, bread and butter to the hungry, and in the barnyard to turn caked udders into bird's nest pies."

Despite the recession, business was not going to the bowwows. Advertisements jumbled pages like broken crossword puzzles. In Venore, Uphemia was "Willing to Care for Respectable Babies." "Rudy, Willimantic's Smiling Butcher" was "Always Happy to Meat You." "The Best and Most Refined People in Connecticut" used "Hosmer's Oleum for Piles." While Lyon's Carbolic Detergent removed "sausage stripes" from trousers, "The Renown King Arthur of the Garden," Selarmo Herbalis, shielded turnips from "children of the moth." "No matter your problems," an advertisement in the Tennessee paper began, "you can always find *sympathy* in the dictionary, but if you are having trouble hearing, try the Dentephone. Doctors will tell you that with a little practice people can hear better with their teeth than their ears." A sketch accompanied the advertisement, the Dentephone being, so far as I could tell, a diminutive metal trumpet, the mouthpiece of which sufferers applied to their incisors or to their canines if the incisors were missing. "Once you own a Dentephone," the advertisement concluded, "friends will say of you what was said of the dumb couple after they walked away from the Court of Hymen, 'they were unspeakably happy.'" This last bit of puff seemed insensitive, at least in terms of ephemeral convention, and after smiling, I felt guilty. Happily, however, a purgative lay but a glance away. At the top of a nearby column, the Church of the Dancing Seraphim in Vonore announced that their Manna Shop had recently received a fleet of small wooden models depicting the Old Ship of Zion, the sails of which resembled wings and the rudders crosses. The announcement urged "Self-Pruners" to purchase models. "Placing them in the bathtub on Saturday night, in the sink when you are washing dishes, and in the washtub when you are scrubbing old flannels will save you from sinking beneath the waves of sinful thought. Like Simon Peter you will breast the Sea of Galilee and sail calm above the stormy temptations of the world, the flesh, and the devil"—in my case especially above what readers who suffer from feverish sensibilities may think devilishly inappropriate. Of course the panacea for that as well as for nasal gleet, barren filberts, and sundry sorts of social galls can be found in. . . . Well, enough; you know where the remedies can be found. All I can advise is that you lay in good stores of particular observation and local reading because in life you are going to need them.

Doing Nothing,
Nothing Doing

"Here you are," **Vicki said,** standing in the doorway, rain raking the fog outside, "a gray man in a moldy room. What are you thinking?" I could have been thinking about many things: Excalibur, the name Edward dubbed the trowel used to scoop dog droppings out of the side meadow; a recent dream in which I underwent treatment for prostate cancer, the doctor flipping radium pellets into my innards like a boy skipping flat stones across a pond; or even thinking about two barns east of Meteghan on Route 1, a stone wall running between them, the paint on the barns giving the lie to Robert Frost's contention that stone walls make good neighbors. "Choose Life," massive white letters on the side of one barn urged, an open hand stretched beneath, index finger extended. Painted on the second barn and facing the command on first barn, the two buildings bookending the wall, was "Barn Again," the letters salmon, beside them a cartoon of Jesus in his hippie, or Woodstock, phase, his eyes a glaze of bleached blue, hair exploding psychedelic about his head in a rainbow of dreadlocks.

I could also have been pondering two stickers pasted on the rear window of a rusting white Pontiac I saw parked outside Tim Hortons on Starrs Road. To the right of the imperative "Drive It Like You Stole It" was a cautionary yellow square advising tailgaters that there was a "Baby on Board." I bought coffee and a dutchie in Tim Hortons and tried to identify the owner of the car. I failed. The only other customers in the coffee shop were eleven men, friends seated around two tables pulled together into one, none of the men under seventy and most at the tipping point of eighty, beyond both babies and a heavy foot on the accelerator.

I might have been thinking about a battered tin sitting on the front left corner of my desk. Vicki bought the tin for two dollars at a barn

98

sale, thinking I would like it. She was right, and when words failed me, I sometimes picked the tin up and turned it about in my hands. The tin was six inches long, three tall, and four broad. Once it held J. G. Dill's "BEST CUT PLUG" tobacco, manufactured in Richmond, Virginia, and "Celebrated for Its Smoking Qualities." The tin was painted gold and yellow, black stenciling running across it, sometimes in curlicues, other times in rows resembling tiles. In the upper left corner of the lid was Dill's trademark, an oval in which a woman leaned backward and stared to her right as if looking at a mirror, her hands behind her head, arranging her hair. Her sleeves were rolled above her elbows, and her blouse splayed open below her neck, low and scalloped, turning her into a bowdlerized Anglo-American belly dancer.

Of course I could have been considering truths, those that the ambitious dare not speak and that no longer intrigued me. I might even perhaps have been thinking about the news, although the world that papers now described was not the one in which I grew up or which I cared much about. No, no, I was thinking about gourds, the sort my grandmother grew at Cabin Hill, my grandparents' farm in Virginia. "Gourds," I said to Vicki. "Rarely do I see them nowadays, and I miss them." Before I could recount drying and polishing them, rubbing my hands over their surfaces almost as if they were pets, Vicki interrupted. "You miss a lot of things, more and more these days," she said, misinterpreting my remark, her tone resigned.

I have grown progressively silent. Much of what I did in Canada was repetitive, turning conversation into a litany. Every day during the first weeks we were in Nova Scotia, I dug Japanese knotweed from the edge of the side meadow. From rugosa roses I pulled fence lines of Virginia creeper. Although the work caused pain to rattle along my spine, my admiration for the plants swelled. I envied their vegetable resilience. Of course time eventually blights all plants. The roses themselves were over thirty years old and no longer blared boldly into a second blooming in August. Instead of downy with lively stems, their canes had aged gray and barren, often serving as trellises for the creeper. Jewelweed took advantage of the dieback and spread through the canes. In front of the bay windows on the south side of the house stood three hawthorns planted by Vicki's parents after the birth of Vicki and her two brothers, Alex and Geoff, a tree for each child. Association with the trees has remained in mind. What has been forgotten is who was associated with each tree. Because he was the second child, Geoff's tree was the middle tree. Vicki, however, wasn't certain which tree was hers, the first or third in line; whether the tree nearest the porch was planted first and thus was associated with Alex, or whether the tree was planted last and was "hers." In any case the tree closest to the road, be it Vicki's or Alex's, was ailing, lichens smothering its limbs. I suggested felling the tree. "No," Vicki responded, "Alex or I might die if you saw the tree down." I almost said, "Don't be silly," but I remained silent, primitive worry zippering my tongue. Instead I cut away dead limbs then, in order to dose the hawthorn with antibiotic sun, I trimmed branches from a nearby maple, overhangs beneath which shadows spread like rust. "That should bolster your immune system, Alex or Vicki," I said, admiring my work before dragging the branches from the maple to the trash pile behind the windbreak.

Not all my dealings with plants involved weeding. For years I struggled to identify a flower growing on a moist bank beside the Cedar Lake Road, initially deciding it was a beardtongue, then changing my mind and thinking it a monkey flower. In August I finally realized the flower belonged to the touch-me-not family and was a garden escapee, an impatiens, a relative of jewelweed, its seed pods exploding when touched, a spring kicking seeds outward, scattering them beyond the parent plant. Flowers on the impatiens, white and lavender and dangling, looked like broad-billed caps on their sides. Identifying the plant boosted my spirits, adding a skip to my step, making the natural world, despite the inescapable presence of decay, more hospitable, indeed friendlier than the worlds described by radio and newspaper. The news always seemed old whereas recognizing a plant for the first time or coming across a "new" fish silvery in a tidal pool, an American sand lance, for example, made living shimmer.

As I meandered doing little, moments clung to mind, becoming postcards of place and season: small pink branches of coral fungus rising Gothic through a hummock of sphagnum moss, the heads of the moss green starbursts; on a gravel road beside a pillow of white clover sinking thumped into itself, spirals of nodding ladies' tresses; behind them four blossoms of New York asters, lavender and yellow; and in goldenrod September heavy sprays of orange-red berries hanging from mountain ash, around them filigrees of leaves, most with fifteen lancelike leaflets, all the leaflets gnawed by caterpillars making them so irregular they seemed handmade artifacts. The berries were edible but, to my taste, bitter, and I spat them out after sampling a handful. A mink wavered across a road while a porcupine jellied through tall grass, its sides saddlebags loose over its haunches. A toad hunkered close to an *Amanita velatipes,* the cap of the mushroom yellow and tinged with red and orange, warts fibrous over it like bits of altocumulus clouds shaken out of textured bands.

This summer fewer birds passed through Four Winds than in the past. Attention is winged, and the diminished numbers undermined exuberance and spontaneity. One night while I stood in the clear dark behind the barn listening to the calls of a pair of great horned owls, a shooting star cleaved the high air, thrown westward toward the breastplate of Hercules. Maybe, to bring old tale to mind, the star was the blood of Nessus burning across the sky, speeding toward the tunic of Hercules. Nessus, the centaur, attempted to kidnap Deianera, Hercules's love. On hearing Deianera scream, Hercules rescued her, killing Nessus with an arrow. Before he died, Nessus gave Deianera a drop of his blood, telling her it was a love potion. He said that if the blood touched Hercules, it would increase his ardor for her. Sometime later, believing that Hercules's affection was waning, Deianera poured the drop on Hercules's tunic. Instead, however, of making him burn with love, the blood ate through the tunic, scalding Hercules and causing unbearable pain. Although Hercules ripped away the affected flesh, he could not stop the pain. In remorse Deianera committed suicide, and unable to alleviate his suffering, Hercules immolated himself.

Early in the morning I watched fog shift from gray to blue then to silver and finally sooty yellow as the sun rose above the horizon. As I walked along the drumlin high above the Bay of Fundy, western breezes chilled my left shoulder while the rising sun warmed my right. Of course I saw some birds: in the mornings ravens, congregations of sea crows, then marsh hawks stalling and gliding low over fields. Later in the day small flocks of warblers trickled through the scrub along the lane leading to the drumlin, leaves shaking about them, the birds mostly yellow and yellow throats, not the astonishing variety that poured through the bush in the past.

One day I followed an ovenbird through alder and wild raisin, the bird's eye-ring piercingly white, its upper breast splotched, the spots not running but clearly defined, a reddish crown over its head making the bird appear startled, its perches tentative. Another day I watched a first fall chestnut-sided warbler forage through white birch, its head and back green and fresh. In September, as I stood under a spruce, a blue jay nattered through branches above me, making a sound I hadn't noticed before, not the high yelp that's a harbinger of fall, but a metallic tut-tut-tuttering, the tuts clacking like brass balls bouncing into one another.

Because jewelweed had pushed aside fireweed and meadowsweet, the number of hummingbirds increased, their chittering and swooping at one another almost ceaseless. In mid-September hummingbirds left after autumn leached the orange out of the blossoms on jewelweed, turning them pale yellow and almost white, the flowers thinning like skin tight across the forehead of an old man.

The population of feral cats exploded during the past year. On our arrival in July, Vicki and I disturbed a gray and white cat living in the basement. For the first time in memory, the house wasn't a granary of mouse droppings. Alas short-tailed weasels had vanished along with the mice, and red squirrels no long scampered across the side porch. On paths I found a score of dead smoky shrews, the cats' playthings, the shrews' fur matted and sticky with saliva. To blame the paucity of birds on cats was appealing but probably wrong. Shore birds were also scarce, the only birds appearing in numbers, herring and great black-backed gulls. Almost no peeps skipped the sand, scouring retreating waves. I didn't see a single ruddy turnstone and only one dunlin and two black-bellied plovers. Terns did not scissor above the water, and just a handful of cormorants sunned on the rocks at Black Point. Loons were silent, and kestrels did not beat the air, from a distance looking like large feathered bees.

One summer does not a desert make. Perhaps flocks of birds will hum through the air next year, but I doubt it, and I suspect that the lives of tomorrow's children will not be as rich in the nonmaterial as mine has been. Still the fallings from sight have occurred slowly, other creatures pulling attention, and concern, away from birds. One afternoon I noticed the track of a turtle on the beach at the Beaver River outlet, probably that of a loggerhead, the markings in the sand heavy and treaded. South of Black Point sand covered the carcasses of two baleen whales, perhaps minkes, the skulls yellow scoops, the wings of the spinal cord of one whale sticking bleached through the sand, leaning into the wind like a fence slowly sinking into a dune. Above the bodies the sand was oily and smudged, the uncovered flesh wrinkled like a shammy cloth. Gulls picked at the remains, especially juvenile black backs.

In great part the air was empty this summer. Few butterflies paddled the surface, stirring eddies of color. I saw almost no white admirals, monarchs, or fritillaries, and none of the usual confetti of cabbage whites. The day after Hurricane Bill rocked past, a wave of northern crescents swept down the lane, a high tide of orange lingering for a week before drifting away. Still I enjoyed pleasant glimpses, the sight of a summer azure on a flat-topped aster, black scything around the forewings, blades of blue fanning sharp from the butterfly's thorax. Moths were also scarce, with the exception of grapeleaf skeletonizers attracted to groundsel near the shed, eight feet away from the tangles of Virginia creeper on which they foraged as caterpillars.

Tachinid flies were probably responsible for the dearth of moths. On goldenrod I found the caterpillar of a brown hooded owlet moth. The caterpillar looked enameled, yellow snaggled along its sides like teeth, a gum line of red below, orange plaque running down the insect's back, black seeping through the color. Attached to the side of the caterpillar was the egg case of a tachinid fly. I saw more caterpillars in late August, this because they had molted into sight. Vests of setae or hair covered almost all of them: the American dagger moth caterpillar, white with long dorsal lashes or pencils of hair; and then tussock moth caterpillars, all common, the banded, yellow with white lashes, the hickory with black lashes, and the spotted, black at both ends, orange in the middle and with white lashes.

Paradoxically the less I accomplished the more I noticed flies: seaside flies on tangles of rockweed and wrack, and scavenger flies that looked like small ants. Avoiding flies was impossible. Inside the house Vicki trapped minute orange fruit flies in vinegar. Outside biting midges, or punkies, swarmed, their bites zinging like weak electric shocks and occasionally raising welts. Some punkies snip a person's skin and, slicing into capillaries, spit an anticoagulant into the cut so they can drink deep. The population of biting midges exploded this summer, and one night in August I counted eleven lumps on the back of Vicki's neck. Hornets also thrived. Bald-faced hornets combed the ground and low shrubs for prey, while eastern yellow jackets ranged higher through the scrub. On some mornings bushes seemed to tremble with buzzing. One afternoon as I thrust though a boggy spruce wood, knocking aside cinnamon ferns and roils of blackberry canes higher than my head, I blundered into a nest of yellow jackets. I heard the swarm before I felt stings—on my left ankle, right buttock, and under my right armpit. Trousers protected me from more stings as I brushed a score of hornets off the legs of my pants. Almost every summer I stumble into a nest. Since childhood I have been stung hundreds of times, but this was the first occasion stinging undermined my enthusiasm for roaming. The stings burned for sixteen hours, then itched for eight more days, waking me in the night. Swelling remained after the itching stopped, the lumps eventually collapsing into hardened lids of flesh, small scars marking the entrance of stingers.

Becoming a tattoo of welts and cuts no longer appeals to me. Eventually the punkies and hornets, blackflies, ticks, and the small dark mosquitoes of late summer wore me out, and I settled into my study, moving my hands only to scratch or turn pages. During Hurricane Bill, I reread *Raffles*, E. W. Hornung's novel published in 1899 and describing the antics of Raffles, a gentleman burglar and master of disguises. After reading about Raffles's slipping the manacles of the bulldoggish Inspector MacKenzie and the arms of the femme fatale Jacques Saillard, I picked up Jack London's *The Cruise of the Dazzler*, a volume in "Every Boy's Library," initially put together in 1913 by the Boy Scouts of America. "The boy," James E. West, chief Scout executive, explained, "must be influenced not only in his out-of-door life but also in the diversions of his other leisure moments." Boys, he stated, were particularly fond of "stirring stories."

In the Boy's Library was a shelf of rollicking standbys, books that I read when I was young: *Treasure Island, Kidnapped, The Call of the Wild, 20,000 Leagues under the Sea,* and *The Last of the Mohicans.* Books on the list were grand summertime reading, and the ten-year-old me would have raced through the volumes, *Scouting with Daniel Boone* and accompanying Tom Paulding as he searched for "buried treasure in the streets of New York during the Revolutionary period." George Custer and Buffalo Bill appeared in *The Ranche on the Oxhide,* while George Washington and Nathan Hale strode through *Tom Strong, Washington's Scout.* Trapping for furs in the "frozen North" with *Ungava Bob* would have been rigorous, but I would have thrived. I suspect that Martin Fuller, *A Midshipman in the Pacific,* would have nursed me through seasickness into healthy adventure. Meeting *The Jester of St. Timothy's* would have been fun, just the thing to lift the doldrums of a rainy day, as the jester was "the smart boy of the school who found delight in 'ragging' his teacher."

Jeb Hutton, the main character of *The Story of a Georgia Boy,* didn't seem my sort of boon companion, but I suppose he would have eventually passed lively muster, for he "had a good head under the sandy hair and a stout heart in his big body." Moreover his doings "were calculated to make the young reader square his shoulders and feel like taking hold of the hardest job he can find." I'm not mechanical, and the only book listed that might have been a chore to finish was *The Wireless Man,* this despite the contents being a "host of true stories of wireless adventures on land and sea, far stronger and more fascinating than fiction." The book introduced readers "to many a delightful character new to romance, the wireless doctor, soldier, sailor, and carried rapidly though their adventures." The book even included a technical chapter that "the amateur wireless operator" was certain to "find invaluable."

Being busy is, of course, a dandy way of doing nothing. Vicki, Eliza, and I spent a day at the Nova Scotia International Air Show at the Yarmouth Airport, the closing of a runway and commercial traffic forcing the show to take a sabbatical from Stanfield Airport in Halifax. We sat in a pasture and ate Paul's fish and homemade chips. Overhead the Skyhawks, the skydiving team of the Canadian armed forces, wove arabesques across the sky, on their parachutes huge red maple leaves. Later the Snowbirds, the forces' flying squadron, flew patterns above our heads, fanning and shuffling through one another like winged playing cards. Two stunt pilots rolled and twirled, climbed, then flattened and fell, waggling their wings. A gold F-86 Sabre dashed across the horizon while an F-18 fighter jet roared by, the sound cavernous, echoing around us only after the plane started slipping from sight. "The World's Fastest Chevy Pickup" raced along a runway, vanishing in a cloud of smoke. Parked along another runway was a hangar of planes, ranging from a huge Galaxy transport plane to a Cessna Super Cargomaster owned by Federal Express. A convoy of military equipment surrounded a field. Quilts of camouflage hung like spiderwebs over artillery. While Vicki and Eliza walked back to the car and read the Halifax newspaper, I went for a ride in an enclosed troop carrier, the last ride of the day. The trip was short, rumbling to and returning from the end of a runway. I wore a red safety helmet and was accompanied by a loud, overweight teenage girl and a grandmother and her two grandchildren, ages four and five.

After the show we drove to Tim Hortons and chatted about the afternoon. I had a dutchie and a medium-sized cup of coffee. Days in which one intends to do nothing lend themselves to spontaneity and are often wondrously satisfying. A week after the air show, I dragged Vicki and Eliza to an ice hockey game, our first, the home opener of the Yarmouth Mariners against the Bridgewater Lumberjacks, attended by 1,117 people. The Mariners played in the Maritime Junior Hockey A League, and none of the players were older than twenty. Teams representing Pictou, Truro, Woodstock, and Campbellton, among others, composed the league. Sewed on the back of each Mariner's jersey was a ribbon advertising local businesses: The Real Estate Store, Garian Construction, Clear Choice Water, and Yarmouth Tractors. One ribbon reminded spectators that Richard Hurlburt represented them in the provincial assembly.

The game was a thriller, the Mariners winning, 5–4, a minute and thirty-three seconds into overtime. We sat along the side of the rink, behind the glass and just above the rink, the bang of players slapping crisp about us. During the first intermission, two contestants threw bundled newspapers at a man standing on the ice. The contestant whose paper landed closest to the man won a six-month subscription to the *Yarmouth Vanguard,* the town's weekly newspaper. During the second intermission the draw for the 50-50 occurred, the prize $598. I bought three tickets for five dollars but, of course, did not win. I have not won a lottery since I won automobile seat covers at a raffle sponsored by the PTA when I was in the sixth grade in Nashville. Eliza and I enjoyed the sporting night out. For her part Vicki said she was too cold to appreciate the game. After leaving the rink, we didn't stop at Tim Hortons. We had gone there before the game, this after eating dinner at Pizza Delight— garlic fingers, Caesar salads, Keith's pale ales, and six-inch pizzas, my pizza a mound of pepperoni, mushrooms, and Italian sausage.

More to Vicki's taste but still to my liking was a day at Bear River, a do-nothing day, not so "refreshing" perhaps as the "circus story" of *Redney McGaw,* but an appealing three ringer. I spent part of the morning watching the tide sweep over mudflats. For lunch we ate black bean and lentil soup in the Bear River Café, the building high on stilts above the river. Afterward I roamed the graveyard behind St. John's Anglican Church. The graveyard had been bushwhacked recently, but blackberries grew near a fence, and I picked a handful and ate them for dessert. Engraved on a nearby stone, a right hand reached down from a cloud, the index finger and thumb grasping a half circle, the broken link from a chain. Later we stopped at the Bear River Vineyard, seven acres of vines rolling over a hillside under a red barn. We bought four bottles. The label on the Greater Yellowlegs Chardonnay declared, almost poetically, "This wine reveals itself quickly on the nose; with a quiet, precise, and rewarding finish that glides through your meal . . . much like our migrating shore bird visiting the water's edge below our vineyard on Bear River."

From the vineyard we drove to the Bear River Exhibition and, to me, something more poetic, the fragrance of manure and hay. We sat on a bench in a shed and watched ox and horse pulls. We wandered through the barns and, as usual, marveled at the glorious size of Belgians and Percherons. At the bake sale Vicki bought a dozen biscuits. Later at home I built a fire in the wood stove, and Vicki warmed and buttered the biscuits for a late tea. Before dusk fog skirted the side yard. I sat in a rocking chair in the kitchen and, drinking tea, looked out the window. The damp had not slowed the hummingbirds. They sliced in and out of sight, chasing one another, their long bills lances. "What a day." Eliza said, spreading blueberry jam over her biscuit. "I'm so tired I can barely remember what we did," I said. "No matter," Vicki said, "we did everything. We always do everything."

Fall

"It was just one of those Malibu nights," Elizabeth Adler wrote in the first paragraph of a novel, "dark as a velvet shroud, creamy waves crashing onto the shore, breeze soft as a kitten's breath." Fall nights in Beaver River are different. In Beaver River waves thump the shore, then ratchet over the rocks before withdrawing, leaving them spackled. In our unheated white elephant of a house, winds hard as shingles bang window frames and hammer through rooms. One night Vicki slept under fourteen layers, eight of them covers, two of these brown army blankets thick as hooked rugs. On her person she hung six layers, the top layer a hooded sweatshirt that Edward wore when he was a camper in Maine. Cold shattered sleep like frost cracking across a windowpane, and I roamed nights, often wandering downstairs and out into the side yard, disturbing deer feeding under the apple tree or at the edge of the meadow, causing them to stamp and snort. The dark was pure, and the constellations so clear the sky seemed a vineyard of story—that of Orion, who so infatuated Artemis, goddess of the moon and hunt, that she neglected to light the night sky. Unsuccessfully the other gods begged Artemis to resume her duties. Then one day Artemis's twin brother Apollo, the sun god, spotted Orion swimming in the ocean far from land. Apollo beamed sunlight on Orion, obscuring his body and reducing him to a blot amid the glittering waves. Artemis was proud of her archery, and when Apollo challenged her to hit the blur distant between the waves, she shot an arrow piercing the target. When waves washed Orion's body on shore, Artemis realized what she had done. Now as grief stricken as she had once been besotted with love, Artemis placed Orion's body in the sky. Time did not ameliorate Artemis's sadness. She lost interest in living, and ever since, the moon has seemed cold and lifeless.

Summer is so comfortable that the eye dulls, the warmth a mist obscuring the edges of things. In fall one shivers and shakes, raises the head, and notices day and season: the sunset, an orange band, below it black jagged cutouts of spruce, above it to the northwest pearly gray, to the southwest a wavering fall of green then a cushion of blue. I wandered early mornings, watching light seep down the tops of trees until it broke and tossed shadows across the ground. In the fall I notice more than in the summer, almost as if I am a wild creature scurrying to build a horde, not of food, but of observation to nourish me in winter while the eye hibernates. The damp woods opened; alders thinned, their leaves seared, last year's cones bundles of small black clinkers. Cinnamon ferns curled ochre and orange, the fronds brittle and more distinct than in summer when they blew limber and green, pulsating out of individuality. Lichens wrapped dead spruce looking like yarn, antlered, hooded, shield, their colors black and silver, brown and green. Old man's beard hung scraggily and matted from branches. At the heathy edge of a wood, balls of reindeer lichens covered the ground. A tamarack stood above blueberry, its needles turning orange, the color flickering in the morning dew. Blackberries vanished, leaving behind leaves peppered with holes and canes soggy and supple. Leaves fell from maples, scooting the air, their stems thin red rudders. Crusts of blue berries hugged bay; and apples were green and red, their shapes creased and pinched, worried looking, not rounded, groomed by pesticides.

Every day I chewed wild raisins. Leaves from the raisin blackened, then fermented, giving the path along the lane an alcoholic fragrance, rich and damp, very different from the drier smell of fall in the deciduous woods of southern New England, this last often making me cough. I stopped and snuffed the air and watched bald-faced hornets scouring mountain holly and winterberry for nectar. In the quiet I often smelled deer. Near fields I heard pheasants battering into the air, the wings sounding like the blades of helicopters. Mornings were chilly, but only my shoulders got cold, and the sight of a bald eagle ten yards from me, floating the air off the drumlin overlooking the Gulf of Maine, pushed temperature from mind. I watched birds: families of flickers at the edges of fields and along the lane; in boggy scrub, swamp and white-throated sparrows; in winterberry a small flock of palm warblers; and almost always yellow-rumped warblers low in the broken spruce deep in the woods, above them cedar waxwings cavorting. A band of twenty blue jays flew high above the barn, jabbering, the flock not shaped like a *V* of Canada geese but swirling, there being no center, the edges crumpling and breaking, the direction appearing almost arbitrary. At high tide eiders, black ducks, and loons fished offshore while gulls gathered on the beach to snag small Gaspereau or big-eyed herring.

The birds I saw were commonplace. What was unexpected were the small numbers, making glimpses special: a Tennessee warbler on mountain ash or a yellow-crowned kinglet studying me from an alder. Summer is a cornucopia, and its offerings are so fatty that one becomes sluggish. Fall raked away excess, almost forcing one to notice what remained. Meadowsweet drifted from sight. Goldenrod turned gritty. Rose bushes became metallic, the leaves plated and coppery, the canes barbed wire, unspooled and rusting. But what was left was more than enough to make the heart leap, especially for the person thrust out of doziness by the cold: bouquets of blue asters in the grasses edging headlands and fields and in wet woods hummocks of sphagnum mosses, their branches spreading and falling, some watery, others cedary, the heads stars or whirling pools, bundles of red and green.

In roaming fall I staved off awareness of my time's passing, forgetting self in the thrill of seeing something for the first time, in the spruce woods a *Zygiella atrica,* an orb-weaving spider, its abdomen jags of black and white, the web six feet off the ground. Under spruce mushrooms were fall's flowers, the abundance astonishing: yellow witches' butter; tiny fairy helmets; spongy boletus; milkcaps, some caps white, others orange or chocolate, but all rising into funnels, the lips rolling over curdled; mealy brown russulas; other russulas with starch white stems and dark red caps; and then, one of my favorites, *Leotia viscosa,* or green slippery cap, a small mushroom two or three inches high, its stem orange, the cap dark green and rumpled, a diminutive of the headgear worn by marshals at college graduations.

Of course one cannot stop time. In the fall, however, time ambled more than it strode. I spent my birthday stacking a cord of wood in the barn. The barn is big and over 150 years old, stobs rather than nails used in its construction. For us the barn is an attic, musty with the detritus of years: a buggy with two rows of seats, a church pew of wooden chairs, fish boxes, canning jars, rigging from sailing ships, a wall's worth of red clay bricks, ribs twisted from the remains of a beached minke whale, ox yokes, doors, a clothes mangle, oil cans, a huge burl, the surface rippled like a woman's hair after a permanent wave, piles of shingles and shakes, cast-iron stoves, trunks, chopping blocks, ladders, oil cans, and a sign reading "The Little Brown Store"—in short the stuff of slow living.

The wood was newly cut, moss and shield lichens still clinging bright to the bark. Most of the wood was maple, but the cord contained enough birch to freshen the barn, a sweet accompaniment to the thrum of carpenter bees that cruised the floor of the loft in the afternoon, rising into crevices between floorboards. Because I had jogged my hip and lower back into pain, I placed a wooden chair outside the barn by the pile of wood. Instead of bending over and picking up an armful of wood, I sat in the chair and tossed pieces into a red wheelbarrow. When the wheelbarrow was full, I rolled it into the barn where I stacked it next to last year's new cord, sitting in another chair while I stacked.

For a birthday present Vicki gave me a painting she bought at the yellow barn in Sandford. A foot tall and sixteen inches wide, the painting was a nineteenth-century landscape, depicting a rugged mountain scene, a lake sandwiched between high mountains, a river tumbling out of the lake ripping trees from a soft bank, above the mountains behind the lake a pale sky streaked yellow and blue. The painting cost fifteen dollars and was filthy. Dusting cleaned it nicely, and we hung it in the back parlor. That night we ate dinner at Pizza Delight in Yarmouth. I had a Caesar salad and a six-inch pizza. Because it was my birthday, the meal was free. Afterward I had a cup of coffee at Tim Hortons before going to see the movie *Zombieland*—a wonderful day, an appealing present, dinner and night out at the theater, all prefaced by the satisfaction of stacking wood, my hands seamed by red scratches.

The next Sunday we ate lunch at D. J.'s Corner Store in Salmon River, our plates mushy with rappie pie. Albert, a ninety-three-year-old farmer living on the Beaver River Road, stopped me at the door. He asked if I lived in the "homestead" across the highway from the Temperance Hall. On my saying "yes," he asked if the man who ran around Cedar Lake "practically every day" lived in the house. When I answered that I was the man, he said, "You look a lot younger when you are not running." Sixty-four years earlier (two years before Vicki's parents bought the house), Albert said he'd papered rooms in the house. The owners, the Beveridge "gals," fed him parsnip stew for lunch. The stew was hearty, and when Albert could not eat a second helping, the two women cried.

Albert's recollection was a fall story, for fall seems more suitable to history than does summer, the shortening days closing down the future and making one mull the past. The cold also whittles at mood, honing the inclination for irritation. Americans are buying the western shoreline of Nova Scotia, north from Yarmouth up the French coast, raising big houses on promontories, reducing the thoughts raised by long open views to eroding ponderings of wealth. Vicki and I are not anchorites, but we are reclusive. We like roaming shore and town by ourselves, not exactly unknown, but unapproachable. In September when we took Eliza to the airport to catch a flight to Portland, a woman approached me and said, "You are Sam Pickering. Aren't you?" The woman had found me on the Internet, something, along with television, that we avoid in Nova Scotia. Although she had spent only three summers in Canada, the woman was an encyclopedia. She told us about people who had recently bought homes in the neighborhood and who put webcams around their properties to protect them against thieves. The woman was pleasant, a summery person, but as information spilled over me, I became irked and distant, resentful that a newcomer knew more about Beaver River than I did. I learned that the man who erected a house on Black Point, a peaty headland over which Vicki and I had strolled hand in hand for twenty summers, was a cardiologist. "Unnecessary knowledge," I said to Vicki as we left the airport. "I'll never meet the bastard." "Not unless you have a heart attack," Vicki answered.

That evening in the kitchen before dinner, I said, "Do you suppose that woman knows bunchberry seeds are yellow? And I wonder if she has noticed crane flies swarming over the grass or tar spots on the leaves of shadbush?" "Probably," Vicki said, adding, "but do such things matter?" "Yes, but maybe not at this moment," I answered, looking out the kitchen window and seeing a doe and fawn in the north field. Vicki turned on the radio. "Autumn Leaves" was playing. "Now then," she said, "it's time for you to build a fire in the stove."

Ports of Call

During the economic debacle my pension flew south and, drifting off-shore, molted, most of its green feathers vanishing in the financial Sargasso Sea. Vicki is eleven years younger than me, and the money set aside for my retirement must take care of her after I'm dead. I don't need to amass more money. What I must do for her is not munch any part of the plucked bird that remains. As a result I will teach until I peg out. When my marbles roll out the door, I will give all students As. Students are a simple, easily-satisfied species, and they will flock to my courses even though I am gaga. Unlike my pension, my salary has remained constant and provides enough for Vicki and me to live comfortably, even for us to indulge our fancies occasionally. Behavior is rarely consistent. The tumbling stock market simultaneously increased and decreased my concern about money. The stability that I assumed the careful accumulation of dollars would bring to the end of life having proved a delusion, I decided to live almost recklessly and took the fall semester off from the university without pay. I explained to Vicki that we'd be able to spend September and early October in Nova Scotia, something we'd done only once before.

Awareness of mortality does not rap loudly at the front door; instead it slices sharp and steely, quietly, into consciousness. Contributing to the decision to take a leave of absence was the realization that I'd become medical bologna, doctors having chopped on me four times in five years, tossing away spatulas of this and that. Moreover I'm the sort of person who once he decides to spend money is, to emend the old expression, "out for a nickel, out for a dime." In past years I lectured on cruise ships. Vicki accompanied me. She enjoyed herself greatly and, during the two or three weeks of each cruise, never seemed to stop smiling. Smiles don't necessarily wreathe the ordinary days of a wife married to a husband who frets about money and, in truth, as he ages, frets about practically everything. To furnish Vicki's mind with happy memories, I booked a cruise on Holland American's *Maasdam*, this time paying for the trip as most cruise lines have cut frills from their budgets: bridge instructors, "Gentlemen Hosts," and "Entertainment Lecturers" like me.

The cruise lasted twenty-eight days, sailing from Fort Lauderdale early in November, covering seven thousand nautical miles, making seventeen stops, fifteen of these at islands, the remaining two in Costa Rica and Panama, all the places new to Vicki and me as we'd never traveled the Caribbean. The stops usually lasted nine or ten hours, enough to allow us to roam and absorb a sense of place. To really know a place necessitates living there for months. The stops were comparable to samples at good wine tastings, impressing the mind and pleasant on the palate, creating an impression and sometimes a memory, both, however, often vanishing as soon as one rinses his mouth before sailing onward to another vintage. To Vicki and me the names of the stops seemed romantic, and before leaving Connecticut, we mulled them, rolling them over the tongue, St. Bart's and Martinique, Curaçao, Dominica, and Bonaire, Barbados, St. Lucia, and the Bahamas, among others.

Our cabin was on A-deck, or four, midships on the lowest passenger deck. I chose the cabin because its location made it practically immune to the pitch of moderate seas. Vicki liked the cabin because she worried about gaining weight. To control her weight she refused to use elevators on the ship and became a stairwell mountaineer, breakfast's being served on deck eleven. Consequently Vicki didn't gain an ounce, this despite chewing paths through both meals and in-between-meals. Cruise lines vary widely. While some lines are expensive, perforce drawing passengers from the comparatively wealthy, other lines run short inexpensive cruises, appealing to the young and people with shallower pocketbooks, packing three thousand people into ships that resemble video arcades, clacking with activities. Slightly over twelve hundred passengers sailed on the *Maasdam*. Almost all were retired and were financially middle class with a parsley of upper middle scattered over the whole. Taking fourteen or twenty-eight days off in November was impossible for most people still working, as it was for the parents of school age children. The average age of the passengers was deceased, as a comedian put it, and a medical supply house of canes, walkers, scooters, and wheelchairs crammed corridors. In fact during the cruise at least one and perhaps as many as three people died, the emergency call over the ship's public address system being introduced by the words "Bright Star." Thus the call "Bright Star, report to Cabin 766" would have meant I was a goner. In fact on people's bemoaning the absence of "Entertainment Lecturers," I explained that economic necessity imposed retrenchment upon cruise companies; on Holland America the age of the passengers forcing the line to carry an undertaker on board, a remark that my auditors never questioned.

I liked the passengers, and almost every night Vicki and I ate with different people. Once politics was ruled out as a topic of discussion, people were remarkably cordial. Indeed one of the major reasons why the aged take cruises is to shatter the isolation of home, traveling on a ship being a safe and comfortable way of mixing with others. A handful of Britons, some Scandinavians, and over two hundred and fifty Canadians were on the cruise, not one of the Canadians from the Maritimes, all from Ottawa and points west. Americans on board came primarily from the South and West, the southerners from Texas and Florida, although these last were grafts, having moved to Florida during or after middle age. Additionally a majority of passengers seemed newly enfranchised, second- or third-generation Americans irked at the government's assessing them to shore up people whose efforts to support themselves had failed.

Vicki and I did not meet anyone from New England. The Americans were stunningly conservative, practically all opposing public health care and most denying global warming. There seemed to be unanimity of opinion on political issues except expanding the war in Afghanistan, this because people resented being dunned to support the conflict. The day before the cruise ended, a Canadian woman told us we were the only Democrats she had met on the ship. The sauna functioned as the ship's Heritage Foundation, the men on its boards always conservative. On some days everyone I met in the sauna had been in the Marine Corps, invariably as enlisted men. Tattooed down one man's left triceps was an M-14 rifle. Often people discussed Sarah Palin's presidential aspirations, enthusiastically agreeing she would make a superb president. I left the cruise believing that America was rapidly devolving into a Balkans of nations. The Northeast would form a union with Atlantic Canada, freeing Quebec to become more French. "Texas," as one man put it, was "already part of Mexico," a region that would eventually be joined by Arizona, New Mexico, southern Nevada, and southern California to form a new nation, "Greater Metexas" perhaps. While the South would go its own bizarre, and probably bloody, way, middle America, states like Ohio, Iowa, Michigan, and Minnesota, would join central Canada. Western Canada and the western United States would then unify, after which they'd level the Rockies, drilling for oil and mining other polluting sundries. The only snares in this sensible division were the Oregon and Washington territories, states that intellectually should be suburbs of Vermont.

Once political hankerings had been scraped away, people came alive, their years rich with story. One woman asked me to call her 38 because she divorced her first husband after eighteen years, the second after fifteen, and booted a lover out after five. "I am sixty-seven," she said. "I have three children and six grandchildren. I had a wonderful career. I made plenty of money, and you can call me 38." "I called the rescue squad when my husband died," another woman recounted. "They arrived and said they would take him to the hospital and try to save his life. I said they shouldn't hurry because he was dead as a doornail. 'You never know,' one of the squad answered. But I knew. What I could not make my mind up about was whether I loved or hated my husband. Anyway, the next day I put his boat up for sale, and soon as the will was probated, I rented the house and bought a ticket to Europe. I stayed two years, and when I returned, I still wasn't sure whether I had loved or hated him. I even sat on the couch on which he died and thought about the matter, but that didn't help me reach a conclusion."

Old friends, generally widows, often take cruises together, but Holland America caters to couples, some consisting of partners but most married, "still doing their time together," in Vicki's words. At dinner one night a woman whose husband suffered from high cholesterol showed me a chart she'd drawn. Her husband liked to eat eggs and bacon for breakfast. "I allow him two eggs once every five days," she said handing me the chart. "The other four days he has to have cereal." The days of the week appeared on the chart; beside each date appeared a "C" for cereal or an "E and B" for eggs and bacon, for example, "Thursday, November 19—C" was followed by "Friday, November 20—E and B." "Henry and I are very close," another woman told me. "One night I dreamed I was walking along a country road. Parked on the shoulder was a John Deere tractor. I climbed into the cab and tried to start the tractor, but the battery was missing and the engine wouldn't turn over. I awoke and sat up, in the process waking Henry. 'Carol,' he said before I could speak. 'I've just had the oddest dream. I was in the woods hunting, and I found a tractor battery. I knew it was a tractor battery even though I don't know anything about tractors. What do you suppose the dream means?'"

"Poor Russell," as I called him, and his wife, Carol, were not so comfortable, especially on the dance floor. One evening a small band played beside a pool. Russell was settled comfortably in a deck chair, and when Carol tried to pull him up to tango, he refused to move, getting, incidentally, my sympathy as I'm an awkward dancer and generally absent myself from the vicinity of pulsating music. For a moment Carol stared at Russell, then she scowled, raised her right hand, and swatted the air above Russell's head, after which she strode off to dance with a woman, another wife whose husband also clung to his chair like a limpet. At the end of the dance Carol returned and standing over Russell, hands on her hips, elbows akimbo, shook her head in displeasure, words falling crisp from her mouth. I tried to hear what she said, but all I distinguished was the word "you" repeated several times after which she walked back to the dance floor, her back stiff, practically a paragraph of muscles, each rippling declarative and scornful. "Poor Russell," I said. "Poor Carol," Vicki said. "Okay," I said, "let's dance." "No, not now," Vicki said. "Well, at least I asked," I said. "Yes, you asked," Vicki said.

A cruise ship is a floating pod or shell, into the upper levels of which have been fitted sundry peas: cabins for passengers, bars, restaurants, common rooms, and a small mall of commercial outlets, the shops attracting the bored. In the mall were an art gallery, casino, spa, and stores hawking liquor, perfume, photographs, clothes, and jewelry, the outlets franchised, their employees not working for Holland America, many not receiving medical benefits and coming from places from which obtaining any job is a boon, South Africa, Serbia, Russia, and the Ukraine among others. In a couple of shops, company policy forbade chairs and stools, forcing employees to stand.

I don't gamble. In fact I so disapprove of gambling that whenever I passed the casino, I turned my head aside. Attitude shapes vision, even when one blinkers sight. One evening I noticed a squat, youngish woman drinking at the casino bar. She smoked and wore black, her dress tight as metal on a fireplug. Leashed to stool on which she sat was a child. "What time does the casino open?" she asked the bartender as I walked past, drink and cigarettes having ground her voice into gravel. I mentioned the woman at dinner. "I've seen her, too," one of my table companions responded, adding, "No one else on board is like her." "She's not happy," the man on my right said. "Unlike us," Vicki said. In truth passengers were remarkably happy, like Vicki and me pleased to be cruising. Every night a show took place in the Rembrandt Lounge. The entertainers always complimented the audience, usually calling them "wonderful," a stock remark but one that was accurate because audiences were appreciative, attending the shows prepared to enjoy rather than to judge.

For their part the entertainers were seasoned cruise ship performers, a comedian telling me that he was at sea forty weeks a year, an aging singer saying she had cut back to four months a year. Some nights the ship's company of dancers and singers paraded wearing huge hats feathery with pink ostrich plumes, just the thing, I thought, to enliven the first day of fall classes at the university. The shows put Vicki and me in high spirits, and afterward we strolled the lower promenade deck, circling the ship, on the lookout for islands and other cruise ships. Some nights we walked a mile; other nights, when winds were hot and stifling, only a half mile. The shows so elevated my spirits that afterward I behaved broadly, putting the featured comedians to shame, in my mind at least. One evening I sat at a desk on deck seven near the shore excursions office. On the desk was a wooden sign identifying me as "Guest Relations Manager." A crowd gathered as I dealt with the complaints of imaginary passengers, saying things like, "No more desserts for you, fatso, only Metamucil." On a man's asking me what he should do with his money, I said, "With a tiny bank account like yours. It doesn't matter a hoot what you do. For all I care you could put it in a saltshaker and dump it on your benazepril." When I started a riff, exclaiming in scornful disbelief, "What—what the hell? You say you are a Republican? Jesus H Christ!" Vicki pinched my upper arm and jerked me out of the chair, pulling me away toward the stairwell before I could continue.

Aging minds do not ponder but work by association. As the *Maasdam* sailed, I remembered the last visit I made to Fort Lauderdale, fifty-one years ago, I told Vicki, when I was a junior in high school. Friends from Nashville and I met girls and were smooching on the beach one night, I recounted, "something that scared us all but Garth Fort more than the rest of us, so much so he raised his eyes from his girl's lips and looking up at the moon said, 'what a great night for tarpon fishing.'" Aging minds sometimes misfire. Later I realized that we had been on the beach at Daytona, not Fort Lauderdale. "A small detail," I explained to Vicki, "not one to which a scribbler of nonfiction should pay attention."

"There is no wealth but life," John Ruskin, the nineteenth-century British essayist, said. For me much of life is winged. I watched turkey vultures settle into trees as the ship left the dock in Florida. Ibis strutted along the shoreline, and cormorants hurried low over the water. Birds people the imagination and, by drawing the eye to close observation, lift thought. I did not pack a guide to the birds of the Caribbean in my suitcase, assuming the ship's library would stock guides not only to birds but also to the region's butterflies, flowers, and trees. I was wrong. The library contained much entertaining rubbish, mysteries and dozy tales of adventure with which to while time away comfortably, but no guides to the flora and fauna of the Caribbean, books that reveal place and contribute to enjoyment. Still, during the cruise I saw many birds I'd never seen before. Some I recognized immediately: on St. Croix, Zenaida doves rufous on the ground; in Panama, black vultures and great kiskadees, their heads of this last black and white Venetian masquerade masks. Brown boobies perched on buoys; while off Cuba masked boobies swirled about the boat, their bills yellow and pinched into lances, their primaries and tail feathers black, the rest of their bodies white washed. Brown pelicans cleaved harbor waters, and magnificent frigate birds beat slow pulses through the high air. On Half Moon Cay, Bahamian mockingbirds called in polyglot amid a scrub of sea grape, silver buttonwood, and knots of love vine. On Aruba a yellow oriole perched on a candle cactus. The bird's head and chest were so bright that my heart skipped. On Curaçao, Vicki and I spotted another yellow oriole in a courtyard amid a maze of tumbled buildings. We started to follow the bird but stopped when a rough man began to track our steps, instinct suddenly urging me to slip away. Later when Vicki asked why I hurried her out of the labyrinth, I explained that instinct was a sixth sense, one that had served me well, protecting me from the inconveniences, and dangers, that can accompany roving.

Glimpses of the natural world served as anchors amid the always dieseling of the cruise: southern stingrays under a pier, corn and curly-tailed lizards, a gunstock of termites packed along a limb, and bats in a high seam quivering like bees cooling a hive. The leaves of breadfruit glistened like rain, and avocados dropped to the ground thumping like drums. I ran my hand over the gray and black bark of West Indian mahogany and studied bougainvillea growing nappy over and through a parking lot of aging trucks and bulldozers, beside the fence surrounding the lot a sign celebrating "Speak the Word of God Ministries." On St. Bart's, Vicki and I climbed a bluff overlooking Shell Beach at Gustavia. Beside the path grew poison manchineel and an acacia spurred with spikes an inch and a half long, the presence of these two tempered by the mild sweetness of flowers on narrow-leaf, or Bahamian, frangipani. At the top of the bluff a green lizard scooted under a rock. A hatching of small orange butterflies fluttered about like shreds of colored newsprint. A thick black bumblebee throbbed across a clearing, and argiope spiders clung to the centers of webs, heads down, legs spread wide, and striped like candy canes.

At every port touts gathered at the dock, selling tours to passengers who had not purchased excursions on the ship. Vicki and I often bought short tours, by ourselves or with two or so other couples, the price at the outside never more than twenty-five dollars a person and half the cost of excursions purchased on board. We rode in cars or small vans, most of which had names painted on side panels or back windows, Peace and Love Taxi, Thanks to Calvary, or The Family Who Prays Taxi. Invariably the tours climbed heights, stopping at scenic lookouts ostensibly far from golden-calf tourist developments and sprawl. The sea lapped distances like blue icing, and islands rose yeasty like muffins, generally looking savory, their sugars untouched by the overbite of rapacious commerce. Atop the bluff overlooking Shell Beach and on tours on Tortola and Barbados, to name but two, I pondered the appeal of high places. Like my glimpses of the natural world, high places may function as some people's anchors. Romantics endow the scenic with the sublime, grand views supposedly raising awe in the hearts, not minds, of observers and unconsciously moving them to awarenesses not possible amid the fret of lowlands and cities. On the other hand perhaps standing on a height and looking to a beyond mitigates the small guilt awakened by the indulgent ramblings of a cruise. On an outlook one can almost convince himself that traveling is restorative, more spiritually so than physically. Actually the cruise exhausted me, and I told people that I looked forward to returning to teaching so I could rest.

After traveling through the early morning on the *Maasdam* as she passed through the Gatun locks in the Panama Canal, Vicki and I spent an afternoon kayaking on Gatun Lake, not far from Gamboa. We hoped paddling would stretch both mind and muscle. We noticed a sloth asleep in a tree, looking like a patch of discarded blanket raked off the ground by a wind, the tines of a tree hooking it out of the air. Instead, though, of seeing anew, we saw the old. Still water behind a small island was a gutter awash with plastic bottles, these tossed from ships moving through the canal. The kayaking was part of an excursion sold by the cruise. I bought two other excursions. They were snorkeling trips, furnishing glimpses of natural landscapes so alluring that for a moment we almost slipped the gangway of our mundane lives, these pocked by habit and convention, and certainly ritual concern, nagging thoughts about retirement, for example.

We snorkeled an inlet in Martinique on the bay of Fort-de-France, near a small fishing village. In part the shoreline was a rubbish tip. Most of the coral was white and dead, smashed by fishing. Along the bottom were wire fish traps and slabs of concrete to which boats could be moored. Still, amid the destruction lay boulders of brain coral, alive and looking rippled by worry. Staghorn coral clumped into nests, the horns proud needles jabbing thick and knitted through each other. Vase sponges collected sediment, not flowers, and sea fans waved delicately. A hawksbill turtle glided away from the shore into the dark blue of deep water. A school of sergeant majors frittered about the rubble, while cuttlefish fluttered stationary, watching me before backing away and losing themselves into translucence. A peacock flounder fluffed into sand and out of sight. A trumpetfish hovered almost motionless, brown and yellow markings making it resemble a file; and a lone banded butterfly meandered slowly along, its black and white stripes wavering, its body a wing catching small currents.

Although I saw many fish, the inlet was an eroded place, its beauty harrowed, not allowing one to escape awareness of hoeing and harvesting. In contrast the coastline around Klein Bonaire, an island just west of Kralendijk, the capital of Bonaire, was a marine park, so well protected that it seemed a natural garden, a field running luxuriant to weed. The coral was starry with color. Beauty invigorates, and Vicki and I snorkeled hard for ninety minutes, never feeling tired. A chain moray shrank into a hole. A queen parrot fish expelled a cloud of coral ground into sand. I followed a black durgon, then small rhythms of blue: blue tangs, purple chromis, and most beautiful of all a damselfish, its back speckled with a constellation of glowing blue dots. A bridled burrfish lurked on the spiny edge of sight. Groupers hung heavy along sand and rock, mottled, making me imagine them lungs. In part because of the marine park, Bonaire became a favorite island, and riding the snorkeling boat back to Kralendijk, I dreamed of spending six months there and writing a book.

The island also attracted me because it was small, 112 square miles with a population of eighteen thousand. In contrast to places that jacked suddenly up from the coast into mountains and rain forest, Bonaire was flat and bare, organ pipe cactus playing dry, simple melodies. Moreover the island appealed to the New England me. Because I live in a temperate zone, corralling temptation and breaking it to the saddle of page and phrase are easy. For me the wild profusion of color and flamboyant, almost reckless, diversity of species on, say, Costa Rica would create distraction and, undermining discipline, foster temptation. On Bonaire the landscape was gray and clear and would enable me to raise blocks of sturdy, short sentences. Climate influences taste as well as behavior. I like nineteenth-century landscape paintings, particularly those hard with bluff and ridge. Occasionally I buy contemporary paintings, these by Connecticut artists and quintessentially local, winter scenes in which afternoon sunlight slips pale over a land bare and blue with cold. When the *Maasdam* stopped in Key West, I explored art galleries. The art mirrored the city, its streets tarty with bars, loud and brazen, its coloration a mélange of strident brightness. In paintings and photographs, light did not consist of spindly rays breaking through trees and shaping mood but instead fanned out boldly, overwhelming the land, implying a Pentecostal sense of gushing spontaneity. Many paintings were cartoons, decadent with martini glasses and the personification of small animals, frequently frogs and toads. In portraits women were often scantily clothed, appearing plucked from a catalog of models flouncing about in foundation garments, then fattened so that their buttocks and bosoms swelled into pomelos. On tabletops dolphins leapt through the glass bases of lamps, while the sculpted faces of children always glowed angelic.

Vicki and I succumbed to the fleshly atmosphere of Key West, guzzling beer and eating pulled-pork sandwiches at the Hog's Breath Café. For dessert we both ate two slices of Kermit's key lime pie on a stick. On Bonaire heat pressed down like a lid, and the streets were silent. I noticed two medical schools, Xavier University School of Medicine and the St. James School of Medicine. St. James was holding a fair in what appeared to have once been a secondary-school building. The building was blue and white and L-shaped, classrooms opening into an open courtyard. Students were giving free medical tests, perfecting technique on passersby. I turned down offers of a dozen tests but chatted in the shade of a porch with three students from Florida. Vicki stood aside, however, and wilted, and soon we walked back to the waterfront and, sitting under palms at Coco's, a seaside bar, drank cooling Polar beer.

Roaming tires. Eventually the grids of cities overlay and become indistinct. As a result travelers remember pauses, atypical moments during which they break their walking and gawking: sipping a ginger drink in Harvey's in Christiansted in St. Croix or a piña colada on the beach at Cane Garden Bay beyond Road Town on Tortola. In Dominica I bought two fruit smoothies for three dollars apiece from "J B The Juice Man," a street-corner vendor. While I leaned against a wall bolting them down, a wiry man with dreadlocks invited me to listen to his poetry, verses he volunteered to recite in a nearby bar. I turned him down and hurried into a bakery up the street, buying a bun speckled with mystery fruit. In Barbados "big mac" took us on a two-and-a-half-hour tour, driving up the coast to Holetown, then turning inland, climbing to a view near Mount Hillaby, passing soft hills rusty with red cattle and fields of sugarcane, the plumes of the grass blowing like banners. At the end of the tour, "mac" dropped us in Bridgetown. After ambling for ninety hot minutes, long enough to set weariness, we went to the Waterfront Café on the Carenage. We sat at an outside table. Henry brought us draft beers, and we ate fried flying fish on hoagie buns. "Life couldn't get much better," Vicki said, as the long bone aches brought on by street walking eddied away.

On walks we rarely met other passengers from the *Maasdam*. In Willemstad in Curaçao, however, after spending a morning wandering the jittery byways of the Punda district, we collapsed at a bayside table in the Iguana Café. To buck ourselves up, we ordered frozen mochaccinos (cappuccinos loaded with heart-massaging chocolate). Sitting nearby was a couple from the boat. "Have you seen the floating market?" the man asked me. Small wooden boats loaded with fruits and fish tramped the short distance from Venezuela and docked along Sha Caprileskade, their decks open with awnings sagging above them. "Yes," I answered, "the shelves of food are a treat for the eyes." "Indeed," the man replied, seeming disappointed that we had visited the market. "Well," he continued, "the market here is nice, but it does not compare to the one in Barcelona. That's my favorite market. You should see it." "I've been there. It's wonderful," I answered.

Most passengers on the *Maasdam* were relentless cruisers, and I met people who had taken more than a hundred cruises. Cruising smacks of the addictive, appealing to the collector in a person's nature, that aspect of character that led me to amass baseball cards in the 1950s. Realizing that once a person takes an initial cruise he is likely to sign up for others, cruise lines work to build loyalty. To lure passengers into additional cruises, Holland America established a Mariner Society, rewarding repeat cruisers with small perquisites and titles akin to merit badges won by Boy Scouts. Thus one begins as a Star Mariner working up to Four-Star Mariner, this after spending 200 days on Holland America's ships. The highest, or Eagle Scout, award brings a saucer-sized platinum medallion, this achieved after spending 1,800 days at sea on Holland America, 26 days short of five years. Rarely do I catch bugs, but, alas, I was susceptible to the cruising flu, figuring that at the end of Vicki's and my trip I would have spent 77 days on Holland America's ships. Moreover if the days I spent on other cruise boats and in times gone by sailing to Britain on ocean liners were added to the total, I would have spent 125 such days at sea, making me a Three-Star Mariner of sorts, rapidly surfing the waves to a fourth star.

Hardened cruisers are competitive. My having been to the market in Barcelona displeased the man. "Now that I think about it," he said after pausing for a moment, "my favorite market is that in Santiago. Since you have seen the market in Barcelona, I assume you have also seen the market in Santiago." "No, I've never been to Chile," I said. "Oh," he responded, a satisfied and patronizing smile on his face, "you must go there. It is quite an experience." He then stood and, turning to his wife, said, "Come along Maureen. It's time we returned to the boat." "Well, he showed you," Vicki said. "Don't play market poker against these folks. They hold all the cruises."

After swimming at Eagle Beach on Aruba, Vicki and I lounged under a divi-divi tree and, drinking Coca-Colas bottled on the island, ate lunch bought from a roadside stand: fish shredded over french fries, the whole swathed in tomatoes, lettuce, and garlic sauce. For a time worldliness vanished, swept away by sand and ocean and a good slow lunch. But then a bingo game began in a resort behind us, across Smith Boulevard, and I heard the caller say, "B 59." The *Maasdam* docked twice at Oranjestad, once on each leg of the cruise, the only port the ship visited twice. Oranjestad itself was rank with relentless souvenir commerce. Still we enjoyed Aruba, in great part because we were lucky, during the first stop hiring Sergio to drive us to the leading tourist sites. At the end of the drive Sergio dropped us at Eagle Beach. Two hours later he returned and, picking us up, took us back to the boat. Sergio was enthusiastic and smart, remembering our names when we returned to Aruba seventeen days later.

Melanoma has slaughtered friends, and Vicki and I behaved cautiously in the sun. We never sunbathed or frolicked in the pools on the boat. During the cruise we swam eight times, these including the two occasions when we snorkeled. We did not linger in the sea, and on beaches and in the water I wore a long-sleeved shirt. Still we enjoyed swimming. On seeing the starched sands and opal-colored water at Eagle Beach, Vicki exclaimed, "This is what I have been waiting for, a picture from a travel magazine." Swimming was also good on Half Moon Cay, a curl of fifty-five acres owned by Carnival, Holland America's parent company. Before swimming, we explored, following the remnant of a trail deep into the brush beyond Carnival's holdings. The trail spiraled, then disappeared, losing itself and us. Eventually we blazed a path back to the beach. I wore shorts, and spiny vines, palmettos, and blades of limestone minced my legs. Blood streamed down from my thighs and soaked my socks.

The cuts were impressive, the sort of thing I'd have been proud of when I was seven or eight years old. Two days later, in Tortola, the cuts became a device opening conversations. After staring at me, several market women approached and asked what happened to my legs. Women even lugged small children over to look at me as if I were an exhibit in a sideshow. In shopping for souvenirs, blood, I learned, is more effective in bargaining than words.

We also swam in Grenada, taking a water taxi from the cruise ship terminal to Grand Anse Beach, a scythe of white sand, tilting above it along the shoreline a dickey of coconut palms. After returning to St. George's, we explored the town, climbing the hill behind Fort George then descending Young Street to Wharf Road and the Carenage. Docked beside the road were fishing boats and a small ferry, grime mottling the boats and their crews. At the Carenage Café, Vicki drank a tropical punch, a mixture of mango, pawpaw, orange, and banana juices with a tot of rum tossed in to fuel the walk back to the ship. I am a more adventuresome gourmand, and I had the "Bull," a blend of Guinness, milk, eggs, oats, peanuts, and sea moss. The waitress insinuated that the Bull would make me kick up my heels and paw the ground. Paw I did not. Snort I did—in nausea. The Bull tasted awful, though I didn't tell Vicki but instead swilled it, exclaiming, "This really hits the spot."

During the cruise Vicki and I spent innumerable hours exploring towns. The digital camera has changed the nature of exploration, so slowing the pace that, for a person without a camera in the company of one with a camera, walking frustrates and exhausts. Vicki took hundreds of pictures, culling them on board at night after the shows. Vicki's mother was a professional photographer, and Vicki was meticulous. Instead of snapping pictures in full quick step, she composed line and shade, shattering rhythm, forcing me to break stride. She lingered behind me. Often I lost sight of her and, reversing direction, circled worriedly until I found her, usually on a street corner pondering field and contrast.

For each town visited by the ship, the "All Ashore Port & Shopping Ambassadors" on the *Maasdam* recommended a handful of stores. Most were generic, a startling number selling jewelry. We avoided the stores. Vicki rarely wears jewelry, never her wedding ring. Moreover I'm not susceptible to the beauty of jewelry, most pieces seeming glitter crafted to attract the simple and worn by the superficial. Consequently the number of passengers who purchased baubles surprised me. Also surprising was the number who admitted being gypped on previous cruises. "I paid six thousand dollars for a bracelet," a woman said. "When I returned home to Toronto, out of curiosity I had it appraised. The jeweler told me it wasn't worth six hundred dollars." "I paid eighteen hundred dollars for a necklace," another woman recounted, "and it fell to pieces just after the cruise ended. Supposedly I had a warranty, but no one answered when I wrote. Eventually I took the necklace to a local jeweler to have it repaired, but he discouraged me, saying the repairs would cost more than the value of the necklace."

Tourism was a staple of the economy of several islands, and souvenir shops flourished around cruise ship terminals, spreading like eczema deep into towns. For the most part the shops sold kitsch and cliché: among other objects, light-up beer bottles decorated with decals depicting fat beaches and jolly whale-bellied sots, coffee mugs, T-shirts, kitchen magnets, sea shells, and rum, this last often Cruzan, the bottles standing at attention in squads, each a different flavor, raspberry, coconut, mango, and pineapple. Crowds milled the shops. Vicki and I, though, usually hurried past, intent on exploring, our general goal local fruit and vegetable markets. Often we were the only cruise passengers in such markets. Three cruise boats docked at Roseau in Dominica the same day, the two other boats each carrying more passengers than the *Maasdam,* one of the boats over three thousand. As a result people clogged tourist sites. The short walk to the Emerald Pool stretched to forty minutes, and the effort to stay on the narrow path without bumping another tourist and tumbling down a slope so concentrated focus that I barely noticed the surrounding rainforest. Many tourists on the other boats were young, and their cacophonous bark and cackle stripped the forest of music. Even worse their shouts of hearty camaraderie drowned the slumberous tumble of water roiling the pool. Later in the day, in contrast, the old market was an oasis, comparatively quiet as Vicki and I were the only tourists wandering the aisles of tables and stalls. By the end of the cruise, however, exploring markets took effort. Being white, and privileged, became burdensome, and I, more so than Vicki, longed to drift anonymously, my curiosity unnoticed and unremarkable, not attracting vendors' greetings, the cries of "Hello, my sweetheart" and "You are my darling"—at first charming but later wearying—making me hanker for the structure and the attendant control of shipboard life.

Vicki and I are not know-nothings or sentimental primitivists who appreciate only the overlooked, believing that truth can be glimpsed solely amid the obscure and unpolished. Our amblings took us though a checklist of notable tourist sites: Fort Christiansvaern on St. Croix; Bibliothèque Schoelcher, the Romanesque library in Martinique; and Ernest

Hemingway's house in Key West, pictures of this last appearing in almost every advertising broadside devoted to and every article written about Key West, practically forcing us to visit so that, when we returned to Connecticut, we could respond positively when people asked if we had seen the house, wondering, as could be expected, what we thought about the "adorable" cats, particularly "the sweet old-timer sleeping in Hemingway's bed."

In Curaçao we went to the Kura Hulanda Museum and the Mikvé Israel-Emanuel Synagogue, the oldest temple in continuous use in the Western hemisphere. Religious institutions attracted us despite Vicki's and my not being religious, in my case outspokenly so, railing against the violence imposed on the world by the three "bloody desert cults," Judaism, Islam, and Christianity. During the cruise I said nothing about religion. Vicki muzzled me, appealing to good taste, saying, "You don't want people to think you vulgar." I am not one of those people who would rather be thought a murderer than a vulgarian. Nonetheless I'd prefer that strangers not speculate about my breeding. Moreover, like the music of Stephen Foster, religious doings run through memory, their melodies often making me pause, even sigh, and, on this cruise perhaps, unconsciously pushing me into churches. In Bonaire, despite the heat, Vicki and I walked to San Bernardo Catholic Church on the edge of town. In Grenada we climbed the hill behind the port to St. George's, the shell of an Anglican church wrecked by a hurricane. I did not expect to glean much from the visits. Indeed afterward I remembered only the small, for example, from the St. Bart's Catholic Community Church, stalks of white lilies in front of the altar, their fragrance dovelike, making me want to sit and rest.

Shopping is fun, focusing meanderings and sharpening awareness, making the wanderer notice all sorts of things in addition to the commercial. While traipsing through and past shops on St. Croix, I noticed a man at the edge of a parking lot playing basketball with a small poodle. When the man bounced the ball, the dog swung in front of him like a pendulum, guarding him. After the man shot, the dog raced for the rebound, corralling the ball against its chest, then dribbling, pushing the ball away from the man, keeping its body between the man and the ball. Such a sight can be seen anywhere. But I saw it on St. Croix, and it made me smile and think the day glorious.

Vicki and I are not ascetics. Christmas was approaching, and Vicki bought presents for the neighbor across the street, our children, and her two brothers and their wives. During the month at sea, we spent $513 on presents and souvenirs, not a bank account but wallet enough to swell our suitcases. Of that amount I accounted for $23. On Barbados I bought a small mahogany box. The box had two drawers, and I told Vicki I'd store paper clips and rubber bands in the drawers. The truth is that after Christmas the box will vanish into the attic. I purchased the box to keep Vicki company and stop her from thinking me a gray man, zealous in rejecting small commerce and silently critical of the fun she experienced shopping. Among Vicki's purchases were food stuffs: lime juice, banana ketchup, vanilla, cinnamon, coconut spice, coffee, macadamia nuts, nutmeg syrup, and hot sauce. I sampled this last in Harvey's on St. Croix. It was so hot it triggered my sprinkler system, causing water to rain from the roof of my mouth. On Dominica she bought three shellacked wooden boxes, on Grenada, six spice boxes woven from reeds. She also bought two tea towels with maps of Grenada green and fruity across the fronts. Coconuts furnished the raw material of several souvenirs: two necklaces, a bracelet, a purse, and a bird feeder. On Bonaire I discovered an interesting crafts shop then became irritated because Vicki spent a lot of time in the store selecting six items carved from gourds: four birds and two boxes with turtles on the lids. In St. Lucia she bought two cloth dolls from a woman standing on the shoulder of a road. During the cruise we saw scores of such dolls. None were as colorful as those Vicki purchased. From a craftsman in Barbados she picked up three dishes shaped like fish, then three smaller ceramics, one in the shape of a sea horse, another a starfish, and the last a flying fish. Vicki bought little for herself, a T-shirt and two bright sundresses in Aruba. As one of Eliza's presents she paid three dollars for a pair of Rastafarian earrings with Bob Marley's face painted on them. Vicki spent $115 in Panama, more than anywhere else, purchasing Panama hats for the boys; a mola shoulder bag and two pot holders; then from Indians a basket decorated with a turtle and green and red butterflies; and finally two woven masks, one depicting the face of a monkey, the other of a coatimundi, the ears of this last sticking up like wire overlooking a red and purple snout straight as a rail.

We flew out of Fort Lauderdale late on December 4. The trip bucketed the sunshine out of my system. The flight was so rough that people were not allowed to leave their seats to go to the lavatory. Necessity forced the man next to me into disobedience. He did not walk, however. He crawled down the aisle on all fours. The next afternoon snow fell, and I shoveled the drive. "Connecticut's sand," Vicki said. During the weekend, artists in northeast Connecticut held open studios. The following morning Vicki and I drove to Woodstock. From Mona Stratos I bought a small oil depicting country winter. A road flowed through the painting, its surface awash with snow. More snow dressed a stone wall and stuck to the limbs of trees, turning them into spare gray whisks. Vicki studied the painting, then said, "Not the Caribbean and coconut palms. Our cruise is over." "Not quite yet," I said. Late that afternoon two Jehovah's Witnesses knocked on the door, both women. When I answered, the younger of the two handed me a broadside and, before I could speak, asked, "Would you like to know the Truth?" I started to ask if she had ever seen a yellow oriole or noticed seedpods hanging like scabbards on poinciana, but I knew she hadn't, so I said, "No, but thank you," and gently closed the door.

Winter Dreams

Early in December a dream so cheered me that I woke myself. The dream was a story, and I wanted to remember it. In the dream a nice but diffident and socially awkward man had a secret life writing comic novels under a pseudonym. Anonymity freed the man from shyness, and on the page his personality expanded into confidence and laughter. The novels made me guffaw, and I mulled turning on the bedside light and recording two or three of the man's good-humored quips. I resisted the temptation, however, because I suspected the dream would have a happy ending. I was right. For years the man had loved the girl who grew up next door. They had played kick the can together and attended the same kindergarten. The girl wasn't beautiful. She was short, and her face was too round, but she was good natured and bright, a lover of smiles and smiling books. She was high spirited and popular, and when the man mustered the courage to ask her to marry him, he was so pessimistic that he was afraid to look into her eyes and stared at the ground. When he finished speaking, the girl snuggled against him and taking his hands in hers, said, "Of course I'll marry you, you goose. I thought you'd never ask. Only one person in the world could lure me away, and I'll never meet him. He's a novelist." And here the girl mentioned the man's pseudonym, not knowing that her old friend and new fiancé wrote books and was, of course, the man of her literary dreams. "Isn't that a great dream, perfect for Christmas," I said to Vicki. "Yes, a bell ringer," Vicki said, rolling away and pulling the covers tight over her shoulders, irked because I broke her sleep to describe the dream.

Apollo sang Troy into being, its towers in Tennyson's words, "rising like a mist." Apollo was young when he created Troy. The songs of the old rarely rise to illusion. Instead they are dirges. In "Tithonus," Tennyson captured not only age's resignation but also its weariness, the febrile exhaustion that makes one long for the snows of oblivion, writing, "The woods decay, the woods decay and fall, / The vapours weep their burthen to the ground, / Man comes and tills the field and lies beneath, / And after many a summer dies the swan." The hereafter of my comic novelist remained a happy, unconsidered illusion. Actual hereafters are not so rosy. During Christmas people write letters describing family doings. Optimism bubbled through paragraphs when my friends and their children were young. Although the activities of a grandchild sometimes wheel silvery down a page, age has tarnished the effervescence of Christmas letters. Martin's dementia had worsened, Sally wrote, recounting that he had almost no short-term memory. "His long-term memory is a little better. He remembers songs. His favorite is 'Danny Boy.' He's still a passable Irish tenor, and he sings 'Danny Boy' throughout the day. When he gets up at night, he sings it. That lets me know where he is, and I can stop him from wandering out the front door."

"For Sally's sake I wish the call of the fields was stronger," I said to Vicki. "What fields?" Vicki asked. "Poetically the barrow but, in everyday words, the graveyard," I said. "Enough," Vicki said. "You need to go to bed, have another happy dream, and write about it." "The trouble with writing is that it leaves everything out," I said. "If leaving things out makes you gayer, leave them out," Vicki said. Happy dreams are the stuff of winter nights, not days. Christmas letters have turned funereal. Moreover Vicki is not as cheery as she once was. Like everyone's offspring, our children have grown apart from us. The sweet, gentle intimacy of childhood Christmases has vanished. The prospect of Christmas no longer makes our hearts leap in spontaneous joy. Instead good mood needs a kick start. To get through decorating the tree Vicki had to slug down half a bottle of Cherry Heering.

Before Christmas, Vicki began calling me "Mr. Morgue." Although my chitchat smacked of casket and embalming fluid, I didn't think myself inordinately gloomy. Still I thought I should be jolly for Vicki and the children. To raise my talk, in the words of the gospel song, "up from the grave," the day before Christmas I went for a long walk in the snow, wandering woods on the university farm. Changing mood is difficult. White caps of snow settled atop the spiny fruits of jimsonweed, making the stems bend weeping to the ground. The beaver pond was frozen. I walked across the ice and, leaning over the beaver lodge, listened at an airhole. In the past I'd heard sounds. One beaver even scrambled up to the entrance of the lodge and growled. This time the lodge was quiet. Overbites of ice hung from logs draping broken and boarded with limbs across the Fenton River. Sometimes the water rushed whistling through them, not this morning, however. A winter wren frittered low and silent along a bank. "Not traveling far or ascending, a bit like my thoughts," I mused. In the woods in youthful days, my winter thoughts scattered in sundry directions, like a flock of juncos bursting quick through multiflora rose. Often ideas shrieked like blue jays looping high through treetops or cutting neat and fast across a pasture like a sharp-shinned hawk dropping from a widow-maker.

The dose of nature did not purge crepe from the season. Fred sent photographs of his and Jane's new twins. "They are lovely girls," he wrote, "though there are a couple of problems. Little Betsy has Down syndrome, and Jessie is bleeding from the stomach. The doctors think they can stop the bleeding, but they aren't sure." I saw Mark on the street. His father was rapidly becoming irrational. "How is he doing?" I asked Mark. "Getting screwier," Mark replied, adding, "early this month he came down with pneumonia. He got back from the hospital yesterday." Mark stopped for a moment, shook his head, laughed silently, then continued. "To get Father upstairs into his and Mother's bedroom, the attendants shifted Mother's bed six or eight inches toward the wall. Even though they explained that they'd return the bed to its original position after they settled Father, Mother was furious. When they left the room to fetch Father, she tried to push the bed back into place and slipped and broke her hip. She went to the hospital in the same ambulance that brought Father home."

"What do you think?" I said to Vicki, repeating my conversation with Mark. "Isn't that a scream?" "No," Vicki said. Vicki is younger than me, and time has not yet pared her concerns down to the medicinal. Indeed my conversations with friends my age are generally, as the old phrase puts it, organ recitals. Two weeks before Christmas I had my yearly physical. On my asking a couple of questions about the prostate, Ken reassured me, saying that most men who lived into their seventies and eighties would experience a touch of prostate cancer, usually something that could be managed. "So much for intelligent design," I thought. That afternoon I repeated the conversation during a jog with friends. "I won't have to worry about that," Tim said. "At my physical the doctor told me my prostate was smooth, the smoothest he'd ever felt in a man my age." "Smooth!" David exclaimed. "Great god! Don't you know that a healthy prostate is supposed to be hairy—bearded and prickly as a porcupine's tail?"

"I don't see what's funny," Vicki said when I recited the conversation. Waking dreams or illusions vanish, but humor remains. Of course time

changes its texture and subjects. An ancient inhabitant of nearby Will-
ington, Connecticut, got up early one morning to drive to the grocery. To
reach the store, he had to drive on the interstate. Shortly after he left, his
wife turned on the radio to listen to the news. An emergency broadcaster
suddenly interrupted an account of Republican poltroonery in Washington, warning local drivers to avoid the interstate, informing them that
a car was traveling in the wrong lane, against the flow of traffic. The
woman worried about her husband, and when he returned home, she
burst out, "Thank goodness, you are safe. I was so frightened. I heard
there was a car traveling in the wrong direction on the interstate." "One
car going the wrong direction! Hellfire!" the husband exclaimed, "There
were hundreds!"

"The old man could be Sally's mother," my friend George said after
I told him the joke. Sally is George's wife, and although her mother is a
dotty eighty-eight and one of her feet is on a banana peel, she still drives,
familial criticism unable to knock her other foot off the accelerator.
"Sally's mother telephoned today, and I overheard part of the conversation," George continued. "'It's not nine in the evening, Mother,' Sally
said. 'It's nine in the morning. No, not the evening; it's morning. Look
out the window. The sun's up; that means morning. No,' Sally went on,
after a pause during which her mother looked out the window. 'That's
not the sunset. What you see is the sunrise. It is nine in the morning.'"

While Vicki transformed herself into a liqueur bottle in order to buck
herself up enough decorate the tree, I tried to quicken memory through
association, turning old ornaments through my hands, among others, a
reindeer that had hung from the cedar trees of my childhood in Nashville, its body wrapped in white like a mummy, a red saddle on its back.
The attempt failed, and I could not raise the smiling dead: my grandparents and mother and father, whose presence I longed to recall every
Christmas. "Don't become morose," Vicki said, swigging Cherry Heering and studying me as I held the reindeer. "I won't," I assured her and
went into the kitchen and swilled an electrochemical cup of eggnog, a
high-octane liver jumper, charged with bourbon, rum, and brandy.

The best way to get through Christmas, Eliza advised me, was to "eat
stuff." I followed her prescription and was in good form on Christmas
Day, bolting a half pound of dark chocolate coconut clusters before ten
o'clock. I'd bought my favorite present at Ocean State Job Lot two
months earlier, forgetting about it until I unwrapped it Christmas morning. I paid a dollar for a Magic Grow Super Snake. The snake was yellow and brown and a foot and a half long. When immersed in water, it

stretched to forty-eight inches. Alas the snake matured slowly, taking five days to reach maximum size. Christmas night I submerged the snake in a washtub in the garage. Unfortunately the weather turned cold, and the water in the tub froze trapping the snake at a disappointing and adolescent two feet two inches. Still I'm in good spirits, hopeful that I will soon have another happy winter dream. Dozing into dream does not come easily, however. The body decays and falls, and after many a year, one doesn't hear the rattling trumpet of the dying swan. The day after Christmas I received a single item in the mail, a broadside asking "Hearing Loss or Just Earwax?" and offering me a "Free Video Ear Inspection."

Actually daytime matters aren't really grim, even if much is "hearse say." Some of the things I am told seem culled from the pages of my comic novelist. The mother of Tim's friend Harry was very old and dying. One Friday in late November she was so near death that Harry scheduled her funeral for the following Wednesday, not simply buying a casket and arranging matters with a mortuary, but also telephoning her remaining friends and relatives and informing them about the funeral. Unfortunately the mother proved inconsiderate, and although she was clearly under sailing orders she was still ashore on Wednesday, forcing Harry to reschedule the funeral for Saturday. "Harry," Tim recounted, "has always been an optimist. Saturday came and went, and the old lady kept breathing. Not until Tuesday morning was she ready to board the Dark Clipper. By then Harry believed her immortal, and I heard he refused to plan the funeral until after she'd spent three days in the undertaker's icehouse."

Brightness is fleeting, quickly falling from the air as Thomas Nashe put it four hundred years ago. Still sparks always linger. Early in February Vicki and I went to the Elm City Dog Show in Hartford. At the show I met my comic novelist. He'd left his pad and pencil at home, so I took notes for him, wandering amid, among other packs, drifts of black Newfoundlands, sweet shops of poodles curried into candy, and Bedlington terriers peering down their muzzles as if searching for pince-nez. I had, to use vernacular appropriate to the show, a bark of a time. A woman leading an Afghan hound rubbed the underside of her dog's tail. "She's being a brat," the woman explained. "At specialty shows she keeps her tail up, but at all-breeds she misbehaves and drops it." "How often do you breed?" a woman asked a man as they stood near a ring waiting for the judging of dachshunds to begin. Frederika, the owner of Thrive Dog Food, a farm in Portland, Connecticut, brought five freezers of "quality meat" to the show: hunks of beef, lamb, pig, goat, rabbit, and deer. For Jack and Suzy, who were spending a dull day at home penned in the kitchen, I bought a present—a chewy costing $3.50, a "beef gullie," the esophagus of a cow. The gullie was orange, almost translucent, eighteen inches long and three wide, muscles curving ribbed from side to side along its length. Frederika said she harvested her own gullies, splitting an esophagus into four strips. Frederika asked how many dogs I owned. On my answering two, she gave me another strip. "One for each of them on Valentine's," she said. This past Sunday was Valentine's Day, and before breakfast I chopped the gullies into sections and gave both dogs a section. Afterward Vicki removed two small bags from a kitchen cabinet. "Here is your Valentine's present," she said, handing me a bag containing coconut clusters. "This is my Valentine's present," she then said, giving me the other bag, this one with eight chocolate turtles inside. "Now, give it back to me and say 'Happy Valentine's Day,'" she instructed. "Happy Valentine's Day," I said as I handed her the bag. "You're sweet," she said, taking the turtles. "Thank you. Happy Valentine's Day to you."

Boring

"Daddy," Eliza said turning in her chair and staring down the dinner table at me, "you are the only old person I have ever really known." Eliza's grandparents died before becoming fixed in her memory. Moreover Eliza grew up in a university town populated by people who left home in order to teach, forsaking place and parents. In contrast the fathers and mothers of my childhood friends settled near home. Like their parents, most were born in and around Nashville. As a result the grandparents and sometimes the great-grandparents of my friends were people whom I knew and saw often. When I was a boy, more old than young people were my friends. They and the stories, both of their lives and those they told, appointed my days and imagination. The doings of some men were practically mythological, descents in sundry underworlds followed by recoveries into near virtue being common. I spent glorious hours in living rooms, mandarins fluttering like butterflies around tall Chinese vases, chair covers ripe with chintz orchards of fruit, on walls family members in gold leaf, their expressions somber, lips pursed on the edge of reproof, and then always, ancient ladies patting me on the hand while looking at Mother and saying, "Sammy, you are the most wonderful boy."

The young me recognized old age as a beloved player in the community theater of my days, a regional theater to be sure, but one that was warming and entertaining. For Eliza old age is almost synonymous with boredom, and in truth I have become bored and boring. Decades ago when I sailed easily above tedium buoyed aloft by a carpet of magical possibilities, I said that only the one eyed and hidebound became bored. I shucked routine as easily as I did corn, peeling away the present, one moment wandering the Grand Trunk Road with Kipling's Kim, the next slogging across the Arabian sands with Wilfred Thesiger. Alas my vision has shrunk; not even the lens of imagination can force possibility into whelping. Moreover I have become immune to the opiates that intrigue and satisfy crowds of people my age—wars, politics, and sports. I never mainlined athletics, but until this winter I ran a handful of road races each year. In November, however, pain began screwing across my hip and winding down my thigh, grinding bounce from my stride. I still try to jog. I am not successful. A woman in a nearby house suffers from dementia. She spends hours scouring her yard. She picks three or four leaves at a time off the ground, after which she crosses the street and throws the leaves into a neighbor's yard. Last week as I jogged up the street, she paused in the middle of the road, leaves in her left hand and stared at me. Plaque smothers her thought like a quilt, but she had mind enough to ask me, "Are you running or walking?" Usually I run with Harry, Tim, and David. They are all over seventy, making me at sixty-eight the freshman of the group. We talk about, as Tennyson put it in "The Princess," "the days that are no more." Occasionally we lament the change counting cholesterol has imposed upon eating. No more can we indulge our hankerings for pork cake. My biceps and triceps, Vicki said last month, have become jellceps. Medicinal matters constitute a staple of our conversation, not a subject that interests Eliza. Instead of figurines, tools, or even books, we collect diagnoses: torpid bowel, fallen womb, deranged kidneys, and disagreeable feelings in the urinary organs and in, as country folk put it, the "prosfate," ailments that rarely kill but that instead are restoratives, invigorating and enlivening our jogs. Occasionally a remark almost makes us skip like fibrillations, David's saying last week, "Life is a tiresome journey, and when a man arrives at the end, he is generally out of breath."

Once the English department was saucy with biting, questionable humor. Now the department bores me. Almost all my friends, old boys of course, have retired or pegged out, their places filled by comparatively young women. Moreover the male English major is an endangered species. "There were so many females and so few males in the building," my friend Josh reported last week after dropping a book off in my office, "that I thought I'd stumbled into the lobby of an ob-gyn clinic." The "new" female faculty members are pleasant and learned, but they don't dither comfortably. They teach and hold office hours, then, instead of "hanging around" chatting and visiting, cultivating the high art of the aimless, they decamp. Two decades ago conversation in the English department was a meandering blend of the light and the heavy, sweet and sour, sharp literary criticism and dull but cheering jocularity. Gone from the department are pranks. The sane male teacher never plays a prank on or tells a joke to a female colleague. Not once in my forty university years have I told a joke to a lady academic. The senses of humor of men and women are irreconcilably different, a lesson I learned and am forever relearning in the microcosmic world of the domestic. Last week before dinner I recounted the conversation of two tailors to Vicki. The men had not met for some time, and on seeing his old acquaintance, the first tailor asked, "How is your business?" "Ah, me," the second tailor answered, "only so-so. How's yours?" When I finished the story, I burst into racketing laughter. For her part Vicki stared for a moment, the slits of her eyes thin as needles, after which she looked toward the ceiling and invoked the deity, a reaction, I am afraid, that delighted me, transforming my laughter into howls and making me ball my hands into fists and beat upon the kitchen table. Although I was silent during most of the meal, puns like indigestion will out. "Did you know," I said putting my fork down, "that after eating the pudgiest daughter of the king of Athens, the Minotaur suffered from the lass-he chewed?" Alas the witticism cost me dessert as Vicki immediately jumped up from her chair without smiling or speaking, went into the study, and turned on the television.

Trudging into boredom has affected the way I read. No longer does implication slow reading into pondering. Instead only quips stop the mechanical revolution of verbs and nouns, for example, Paul St. Pierre's warning readers in the introduction to *Breaking Smith's Quarter Horse*, "If there is a moral in this book, it is not my fault." I have also forsaken spading about in poetry to unlock the "energy," to paraphrase Marianne Moore, in a "work of art." Now I enjoy poems that tell simple stories, sappy and often lugubrious stories, indeed moral stories in contradistinction to St. Pierre, stories that seem true to my immediate experience but that strike the young and the subtle as boring, even stupid. To find such poems I explore neglected nooks of the university library, almost the literary equivalent of slow jogging, the kind of ambling that cannot be distinguished from walking. Recently I thumbed twenty years of the *Rural New Yorker*. In the number for January 1883, one of my sorts of poems appeared in "For Women," a column edited by Miss Ray Clark. The poem consisted of four stanzas, two of which I read to Vicki at dinner.

> I have a lock of flaxen hair
> Wrapt in a tiny fold.
> 'Tis hoarded with a miser's care.
> 'Tis dearer than gold.
> To other eyes of little worth

Yet precious unto mine;
For once, dear child in life and health,
It was a lock of thine.

The numbered hours pass slowly;
Days, weeks and months depart,
And still the vacant place remains
Unchanged within the heart.
The loneliness is still the same.
The same great want is there,
While memory loves to brood upon
The simple lock of hair.

I haven't completely rejected profound poetry. In class I often quote *Paradise Lost*. However I alter the verse slightly in order to make Milton more accessible to students, for example, emending "Hail horrours, hail / Infernal world, and thou profoundest Hell / receive thy new Possessor: One who brings / A mind not to be chang'd by Place or Time" so that Satan's words read, "Howdy do horrors, howdy / Do Infernal world. / I hope you don't mind if I come in and visit for a spell. / I'm not a bad sort just a little set in my ways." In class I quote often. Occasionally my attributions are wrong, an inconsequential matter as students are usually too bored to notice. Last week I attributed "Whatsoever ye would that men should do to you, do ye so to them" to Uncle Joe Stalin. Actually Janice was awake and corrected my error, attributing the words to George Washington, "the father of this great Republican country of ours." "Republican country of yours," I replied, correcting her presumption.

Unlike teachers, students are not boring. Last month a student in my course devoted to American nature writers recounted that he "enjoyed exploring the woods with a friend and listening to the giggle of the deer." "I applaud your adventuresome spirit," I wrote on the margin of his paper. "To pursue *Odocoileus virginianus* so deep into its lair that you are able to eavesdrop on conversation is admirable. But let me suggest that during hunting season you avoid the forest, particularly if your sidekick is prone to jocosity. A single guffaw might lead to tragedy." On Tuesday in the nature writers class, an aspiring biologist described the tongue-eating louse, a parasitic crustacean. After swimming through the gills of the spotted rose snapper, the louse attaches itself to the fish's tongue. It then extracts blood from the tongue using its claws. Eventually the tongue withers, whereupon the louse binds itself to the stub of the tongue, becoming, in effect, a lingual prosthesis, feeding upon mucus in the mouth of the fish while enabling the fish to continue eating almost as if it possessed its original tongue. After listening to the description of the louse, Alton, a lively B-minus student, waved his arms above his head and exclaimed, "Praise the Lord. Until this moment I was an atheist. But now I believe. Only a god could create such a marvel."

The Internet has expanded both the classroom and the teaching day. Elementary and high school students who once wouldn't have stumbled out of anonymity because writing letters is a chore click out swarms of e-mails. At term paper time I receive pods of such mail asking the same questions: "Who were your role models?"; "Who is your favorite author?"; "Where do you write?"; and, if the student lives in the old Confederacy, "How has being a southerner influenced your writing?" I think all celebrity unappealing, even the criminal variety, and because I no longer hanker to appear in a television exposé, my replies are studiously boring. Being boring can be beneficial. At best it is medicinal, blocking the alphas and omegas of suspect liveliness. Late last semester I answered a catechism of questions sent to me by Bootsy, an eighth grader living in West Texas. Josh happened to come by my office and see my responses on the computer. "You are so boring," he said, sitting down and composing a reply on a piece of scratch paper. "Send this instead of your answers," he said. "It's how a good southerner would reply." "Dear Bootsy," I did not write, "You say you just celebrated your twelfth birthday. I bet you are sweet. Twelve is my favorite age. I was a nice little boy when I was twelve, and I am still a nice little boy although I look a teeny-weenie bit older now. I wish I could have come to your party. I would have brought some ice cream. I would have brought strawberry. Do you like strawberry? Or perhaps you like bubble gum and moon mist better—ooh! Maybe we can meet next year on your thirteenth birthday. You could catch a bus in Midland, and I would meet you at the bus station in Texarkana. Wouldn't that be funsy-onesy? I will bring a special cake and some special ice cream. Don't tell your teacher where you are going. Let it be a big, big, big surprise."

If prose can be a diagnostic indicator, then Josh suffers from ice creamitis. That aside, however, as one's memory fails, chances are good that he will become boring. The same day I answered Bootsy, I received a letter from a former student. "I just wanted to thank you once again for your inspired teaching," he wrote. "The more I see, the more I realize how important it is to have good professors teaching the next generations about the beauty, majesty, and importance of Nature. I look forward to picking up the torch and running with it." "Great god!" Josh exclaimed after plucking the letter from my desk and reading it. "Who is this literary incendiary?" "I don't know," I said. "Well, when did you teach him?" Josh continued. "He says last spring," I replied, "but I don't remember him." "Oh, dear," Josh said. "I am afraid you are heading for everlasting boredom."

In January I dreamed I attended a stranger's funeral. The dead man and his wife had not spoken to each other in thirty years. No one at the funeral knew why the couple had stopped speaking, and later that morning after breakfast, I mulled the matter. Certainly nothing important triggered the silence. Big matters demand words. What small thing, I wondered, led to the silence, and when did the couple know they were behaving foolishly—after three hours, a day, two weeks? When did they reach the point at which they concluded that breaking the silence would render their behavior absurd and their lives meaningless? I couldn't reach any answers, so I stopped thinking about the couple and ambled into the kitchen. Vicki was making a cake for Eliza's birthday. "I've been up a while," I said, "and thought I'd come and visit with you. Is that all right?" "Marginally," Vicki said. Behind Vicki's tepid response was the realization that eventually I'd pun. According to Josh, excessive punning is a symptom of marital Asperger's, a condition arising after people have been married for decades and who, having "talked too much," are beginning to think each other boring. In any case, shortly after sitting down, I rose yeasty, like Vicki's batter, to a scrumptious pun. "What piece of music," I asked, "does an excessive tobacco masticator bring to mind?" On Vicki's remaining silent, I supplied the answer, "An overchewer, of course."

At times I worry that being boring is a symptom of the ailment "all played out." Intellectual exhaustion undermines cultivating unknowing. When a person is too weary to mull, simplicity becomes seductive, and if one is not attentive, he can slip easily into being opinionated. Instead of dosing with Nervine to counteract the metastasizing of opinion, I try the natural remedy of startling myself. In class I ask unexpected questions—what, for example, did the dragon eat and drink before slinking out of his cavern to fight St. George? Sometimes I lie. "Did you know," I asked my class last week, "that Woodrow Wilson kept the embalmed corpse of his great-aunt Abigail in an armoire in the attic of the White House?" Mind you, my lies are transparent. Every schoolboy knows that James K. Polk, not Wilson, stored his great-aunt in the attic, and her name, of course, was Gretchen, not Abigail.

I haven't completely given up dreaming of finding, as the saying puts it, "an egg within an egg." One morning in February I roamed the banks of the Fenton River at dawn. I hoped glimpses of the natural world would jump-start my imagination, causing the flat line of boredom to waggle and jitter into peaks and valleys. Alas the Connecticut landscape is not enchanted. Stone walls crumble, and foundation holes gap, periwinkle burring green around some, but a person sees so clearly he sees little. He never stumbles upon a sacred grove. When he kicks leaves aside, he turns up granite till, not smashed lintels or arches, the remnants of almost forgotten cities and the abodes of ancient gods. Deer and all-terrain vehicles cut paths through the woods, not pilgrims wending ways to ancient shrines searching for cures for tooth- and heartaches, asking goddesses to bring barren fields and women into fruition. To me the landscape appeared old and enervated. Wracks of branches slowed the pulse of the river. Field grasses fell over, white and tottering, while a parchment of frost covered the ground, its texture rough, rising irritated into small, thin spikes. No matter their actual size, white oaks looked stubby, like the blotched, bloodless legs of tired men. White pines lay broken across hillsides, bark unraveled, limbs jabbing up sharp, appearing shaved, turning the trunks into medieval weapons, massive wooden porcupines to roll down a hill at an approaching enemy. Mourning doves wailed, their laments, I thought, caused by the loud monotony of cardinals, their songs clanking incessantly.

This past week Edward drove home for Easter. Shortly after his arrival, while I was scooping dog candy from the front yard, Edward tried to explain deixis, a fancy word describing linguistic doings. "You are not paying attention," Edward said. "Something Ray told me Friday interests me more." "What's that?" Edward asked. Ray's mother-in-law is ninety-two and lives alone in Rhode Island. Last month when her microwave oven died, she called Joan, Ray's wife, and asked her to select and buy a new oven for her. Ray consulted *Consumer Reports*. Because a branch of Home Hardware is located a block away from his mother-in-law's house, Ray drove Joan to the Home Hardware store in Manchester, Connecticut, so she could examine the oven recommended by *Consumer Reports*. "The microwave seemed perfect," Ray recounted, "not only that but the store in Rhode Island had several units in stock." Instead of immediately buying the oven, Joan delayed, deciding to purchase a unit at the store near her mother's house, thinking that if the oven turned out to be faulty or broke before the warranty expired, "getting it replaced would be easier if it was bought in Rhode Island rather than in Connecticut." The next day Joan drove to Rhode Island and purchased a microwave. "I didn't go to Home Hardware. I went to a local store," she reported that night at dinner, handing Ray her receipt. "This is fifty dollars more than the price quoted to us yesterday," Ray said. "I know," Joan said, "and I did not buy the oven recommended by *Consumer Reports*."

"What did Ray say then?" Edward asked. "Nothing," I said. "What!" Edward repeated, the word an exclamation, not an interrogative. "Plant a smile of good temper on your face and root out all angry feelings," I said quoting an old saying as I tossed the candy into pachysandra by the driveway, "and you will reap a good crop of happiness or at least peace of mind," the last phrase an addition of my composing. "What," Edward said again, eyes beginning to glaze over. "Don't forget," I continued, "that a slip of the foot is safer than a slip of the tongue." I had just started scratching about. That morning I'd gone to the Southern New England 4-H Poultry Show held in an arena at the university, and I imagined goings-on at the show might interest Edward. They didn't. Saying he had to review a book, he turned and walked into the house. Too bad, now he will probably never know that chickens with red ear lobes lay brown eggs while those with white lobes lay white eggs. What would he have thought on learning that chicken nuggets were among the snacks sold at the show? When he returns to New Haven, he won't be able to lop the head off literary cackling by interrupting and informing auditors that although most chickens have four toes, Silkies have five.

Afterword

Last Saturday was gray, the snow thin and hard across the yard, rising into brown welts at the edge of the road. Silence was rusty and thick. Squirrels stayed in their nests and didn't scribble through trees. I watched an oak leaf drag across the ground, staggering and shuffling as if on crutches. Chopping fruit into bites and dumping them into a bowl of granola seemed work, and I skipped breakfast. Vicki asked if I wanted to accompany her to the biannual book sale at the Mansfield library. In the past I enjoyed the sale and, when in Connecticut, never missed it. This time I pouted and refused to go, saying, "Repetition used to be comforting and assuring. Now it's irritating." After Vicki left, I felt guilty, so I wrapped myself in coat, scarf, gloves, and two stocking hats and, going outside, scraped dog droppings off the snow, tossing them into a rumple of periwinkle. While in the yard, I mulled the conclusion to this book. "Instead of an afterword," I thought, "I'm going to write a farewell to writing." Last week in rejecting one of my essays, an editor called my writing "completely charming." "I'll bottle the sweat charm wrings out of my hide," I muttered. "Next I'll lament having earned only pizza money from my books, and plain pizza, too, without mushrooms or pepperoni," I said aloud. "And," I concluded, "I'm tired of being reckoned an amiable buffoon. I'll show readers that the person they think a hamster is actually a bushmaster."

"I'll have to work on that last analogy," I thought, as I turned toward the back door. Happily indulgence had warmed me and the day, and I noticed a nuthatch spinning around a maple, jabbing the bark searching for insects. "Bon appétit, pal," I said. When Vicki returned from the sale, I was finishing breakfast, granola buried under fields of strawberries and blueberries, the whole atop a banana plantation. "I've brought you a couple of treats," she said, "a cranberry muffin and a slab of fudge. Which one do you want?" "I'll eat both right now," I said, pushing the cereal bowl aside. Shortly afterward my friend Josh telephoned. He'd seen Vicki at the library, and he wanted to tell me about the sale. He didn't buy any books, but he noted two titles, both numerological, *A Thousand Days in Tuscany* and *26 Minnesota Writers*; the first book, he said, 998 days and 320 pages too long, the title and the contents of the second "canners even if split in half to produce two primes." What local Republican, Josh speculated, had owned *The Goebbels Diaries, 1942–1943* before donating it to the sale? Josh kept an eye on the book. "Doing my civic duty," he explained. "The person who purchases the book merits observation, if not reporting." Actually Josh himself deserves watching. He discovered two copies of *Male Sexuality* for sale. On the inside cover of the volumes, he wrote the names of their previous owners, attributing the ownership of one book to a man, the other to a woman. "Giving the two prissiest, old-maidish nincompoops on the Mansfield Town Council secret lives," he said. Josh also found and inscribed one of my books. "I jacked the price up from one dollar to four," he reported, "and on the title page wrote, 'whoever buys this book is one goddamn smart son of a bitch,' after which I signed your name."

Although the hounds of spring still shivered in their kennel, Josh's conversation raised my spirits, and sassy summer blossomed in imagination and on the page. In fact the previous day a reader had sent me a springlike couplet, one I'd initially thought corny, but which now made me smile. "'Tis wheat to n-oat the progress of the approach of spring. / Onion-der hills and meadows nature is bean arrayed in all herb beauty." My correspondent enjoyed puns and ended by observing that sophisticates schooled in the language of diplomacy referred to a dogfight fought over the affections of a "mongreless" in season, as "an affaire du coeur."

I realized that reporting such correspondences might provoke an occasional reader to shout "farewell" and abandon my writings, especially a reader who believed *Male Sexuality* a "must read." For my part, however, the afterword suddenly became a continuance of paragraphs, work appropriate for a "Man of Letters." Many people write me, the matters of their letters as diverse and colorful as summer flowers. "My husband's sister chews her soup. The kind doesn't matter—lentil, tomato, or pea. She chews it," a woman wrote from north Georgia. "Even worse, every year we go to her house for Christmas dinner. For dessert she serves homemade cookies, not sugar cookies or Viennese crescents, but terrible, terrible cookies, this past holiday clam cookies, the chopped clams looking like earthworms. Last year she served broccoli cookies, and the year before cauliflower cookies covered with cheese. And she raises white mice that she skins and sews into caps then gives to me and my husband expecting us to wear them. Whenever I go to the grocery, I have to carry my hat in a bag so that I can slip it on if I see her." The woman begged me for advice, saying that, although she loved her husband, his sister was driving her to despair "and ulcers." I considered advising the woman to ask her pharmacist for "a dozen of his best pills," thinking my reply might mystify her into calm. I haven't answered the letter. Sometimes answers don't come easily.

Fortunately most letters don't require therapeutic responses. On my desk lay a poem sent from a man in assisted living in Coral Gables, Florida. The man said that years earlier he had copied the poem out of a nineteenth-century periodical. He had forgotten the journal but thought it had something to do with farming.

> The Black Monkey sat up in a tree.
> The Black Monkey he grinned at me.
> He put out his paw for a coconut,
> And he dropped it on my occiput.
> The occiput is a part, you know,
> Of the head and is sensitive to a blow,
> And it is very unpleasant to have it hit,
> Especially when there is no hair on it.

Not all mail I receive is lighthearted. Much startles, however. Another resident of assisted living wrote me from Wilmington, North Carolina. The man was an emeritus professor of history. In perusing reports of debates in the North Carolina legislature, he'd run across references to a bill introduced by a member from western North Carolina in 1891. The bill attempted to limit medical expenses, "a matter," my correspondent said, "still infecting headlines." The bill read, "It shall be unlawful for any doctor or doctors to charge over $25 for cutting a person open and taking abscesses out of them." Grimmer was the clause declaring, "It shall be unlawful for any doctor or doctors to charge over $5 for any labor case, except when he has to take the child from the woman by pieces, then he shall be allowed to charge $7.50."

Many of my correspondents clip newspapers. From Arkansas a woman sent a Christmas story that appeared in her small town paper, the header above reading "Merchant Gives Armchair to Amputee." An employee of the local power company had been electrocuted while repairing wires knocked down by a tornado. In the accident the man lost both arms, and the headline above the account of the gift, though well intentioned, was, to say the least, phrased inelegantly. A member of a congregation in Pennsylvania that seceded from the Episcopal communion sent a copy of the marriage vow now used in her church. "Wilt thou have this Woman to thy wedded wife, to live together after God's ordinance in the holy estate of Matrimony? Wilt thou love her, comfort her, honor, and keep her in sickness and in health; and forsaking all others, keep thee only unto her, so long as ye both shall live, no matter that the President is a Democrat?" From Anniston, Alabama, a woman wrote, describing a speech in which a candidate for the senate pledged that he "would vote in favor of the next war."

Winter keeps many people housebound and is responsible for polysarcia and letters. My mail bloats, and I sometimes think that for numbers of people the only alternative to eating is writing me, especially folks beyond thinking knees look like apple dumplings. Still the letters melt the melancholy that sometimes chills the heart, and they make me want to scribble on until I fall off the twig. Occasionally they even contain antidotes for spleen and wintry dissatisfaction. This past Monday I received a packet containing four handkerchiefs, each in a separate sandwich bag. The woman who sent the packet had perfumed the handkerchiefs. "I made the scents myself," she wrote, "yellow jasmine and clover blossom, wild olive and sweet briar. Spring is only a breath away."

About the Author

SAM PICKERING is a native of Nashville, Tennessee. He has spent sixty-five years in schools, wandering classrooms in the United States and in sundry outbacks over the seas. For the past three decades he has taught English at the University of Connecticut. Pickering is a member of the Fellowship of Southern Writers and is a graduate of Sewanee, Cambridge, and Princeton. *Dreamtime* is his twenty-fifth book.

CPSIA information can be obtained at www.ICGtesting.com
Printed in the USA
LVOW112044250911

247767LV00005B/1/P